GILGAL TO BETHEL

GILGAL TO BETHEL

NICO SMIT

Copyright © 2025 by Nico Smit

Nico Smit's blog: nicosmitblog.com

All rights reserved. No part of this book may be reproduced in any manner whatsoever without written permission except in the case of brief quotations embodied in critical articles and reviews.

First Printing by Ingram Spark, 2025
ISBN: 9781763547698
eISBN: 9781764124706

Scripture taken from the New King James Version®. Copyright © 1982 by Thomas Nelson. Used by permission. All rights reserved.

Published by Bekker Media on behalf of Yeshua Collective, Pty Ltd,
58 Channel Highway, Kingston TAS 7050.

Cover design by Matthew de Livera, @mdfilmcreative
Edited by Bekker Media, New South Wales, Australia
www.bekkermedia.com

Contents

Endorsements		vii
Foreword		xi
	Introduction: The Journey Beyond Salvation	1
1	Salvation Is Out Of Egypt—Sanctification	9
2	The Road To More Is Through Surrender	17
3	The Manna Mentality Must Die	29
4	Gilgal – The Place Of Cutting	37
5	Jericho – The Place Of Obedient Faith	45
6	Ai – The Place Of Defeat, Repentance, And Worship	59
7	Bethel – The Place Of Habitation And Worship	69
8	From Miracles To Blessing	77
9	Possessing Your Possession	87
10	Crossing The Jordan–Stepping Into The Supernatural	97
11	Occupy Or Visit?	109
12	Kingdom Not Crisis	121
13	Habitation Over Hustle	133
14	From Promise To Fulfillment	143

15	Conclusion: It's Time To Advance	153
	Other Books By Nico Smit	157

Endorsements

I have loved reading Ps. Nico Smit's new book *Gilgal to Bethel*.

Now, I'm a grace and faith preacher, so I love it when I read that it's all about Jesus and His finished work - not *our* efforts, striving and performance! I love quotes from Nico's book like this one: "God is searching the earth for those who will yield. Not perform. Not strive."

Good on you Nico for nailing it, it's not by might nor by power BUT by His Spirit!

"It is a call to abandon the "manna mentality" that lives from moment to moment, barely holding on, and embrace instead a life of overflow. Not by striving, but by surrendering. Not by performance, but by presence. Not by earning, but by abiding." (Quote).

We certainly need 'Revival' or 'Renewal' in Australia, but for it to be the genuine article it needs to be God's Way, not 'man's way', or pure emotional response through 'hype' and self-efforts!

"A manna mentality makes people act entitled, with demands, rather than seeing God's wonderful opportunities. It makes Christianity about waiting for God to show up, instead of realizing that He already has." (Quote).

Dr. Col Stringer, Gold Coast, Australia
International Preacher, Author and pastor
Col Springer Ministries

I am so blessed by the ministry of Ps. Nico Smit! He is a devoted follower of Jesus and a committed builder of His Church. His ministry is marked by a deep love for God's Word and his unwavering commitment to shepherding others with grace and truth. His writing, whether books or blogs, is always theologically rich and practically relevant; infused with truths directly from Holy Spirit, Himself.

In *Gilgal to Bethel*, Nico describes how the journey the Israelites took through the Promised Land mirrors that of the believer today. Our own journey of sanctification is a process marked by faith, obedience and worship to enter our own promised land. The Spirit within you will leap through these pages and refresh you anew to further press forward on the beautiful journey with Him from promise to fulfillment.

Daniel Meyer, USA
Broadcaster, Pastor and Prophetic Voice
Founder of Watchmen on the Wall Channel
YouTube @watchmenonthewall

Each time I pick up a book that has been written by Nico Smit, I hear the word 'please fasten your seat belt low and tight'.

That is because there is turbulence, and that turbulence is usually in my mind. His latest book *Gilgal to Bethel* is no different. There will be a turbulence as you allow yourself to travel through the whirlwind of thoughts, letting new thoughts replace old thoughts. It is a journey of transformation. It is a journey of redemption. It is a journey of Love. Thank you, Nico, for your faithfulness.

Hugh Marquis, Adelaide SA, Australia
Author, Prophetic Minister, Inventor, Social Change Philanthropist and Entrepreneur
Pioneer at Live to Love.com.au
Board member Iris Global Board and Harvest International Ministries
CEO at Transformational Leadership Australia

Discover groundbreaking transformative work with Ps. Nico Smit's, *Gilgal to Bethel*.

This essential guide is designed for anyone seeking deeper spiritual growth and a more fulfilling Christian life. With profound clarity and eloquence, Nico offers a daily roadmap to holiness and surrender, helping readers move beyond mere survival into a thriving existence in the Kingdom of God.

Each chapter reveals simple yet profound insights that challenge your perspective, inspire change, and encourage spiritual growth. This book is more than a collection of words; it's a spiritual encounter that will reshape your inner world, blending practical wisdom with divine guidance.

Nico invites readers to leave behind the "Manna mentality" of scarcity and embrace the abundant "Promised Land mindset." His fresh perspective illuminates the path to a life of purpose and passion, reigniting your faith and strengthening your connection to God.

Gilgal to Bethel is a book to be savored slowly, allowing its truths to take root and transform your heart.

Ps. Nico Smit's voice stands out as a beacon of hope for a generation longing for spiritual renewal. Join the movement toward a vibrant, dynamic Christian journey. Let this book inspire you to step into a life of abundance, faith, and purpose. Your transformation begins here.

Dr. John Varughese
Theologian, Teacher and Pastor
Dean of International Affairs, Covenant University, Hudson, FL
Lead Pastor, Evangel AG Church

Gilgal to Bethel is a panoramic journey of transformation that takes the believer through all the stages of maturing in Christ. From a new babe in Christ to a fruit bearing, destiny walking, mature saint who is living a victorious Christian life.

This book will give clear insight and spiritual nuggets to help every believer navigate all the growing pains of the Christian life, while also equipping them with tools needed to *be "more than conquerors through Christ who loves us."* (Romans 8:37)

A must read for all believers and leaders. A highly recommended resource.

Jimmy NJino, Toowoomba QLD, Australia
Pastor, Prophet and Teacher
Senior pastor at Victory Life Toowoomba
Member of the Australian Prophetic Council

This is it! My friend Ps. Nico's book *Gilgal to Bethel* is a road map for any believer's sanctification journey. I wholeheartedly endorse it!

Gilgal, the place of transition after crossing the River Jordan, marks the shift of the Israelites moving from fugitives to inheritors. Beth-el is the sacred House of God which Nico urges us to enter. It is kingdom life under the King's reign that is not meant for beggars but for mature saints in kingdom partnership with God.

This book points readers to circumcise (cut) our hearts, rolling away our hidden things and mountains, so that we may enter our next level of God's supernatural. Do not miss this important book. It will help shape daily blessed lifestyles for today, for tomorrow and for many years to come.

Rev. Dr. Jeremiah Yap, Kuala Lumpur, Malaysia
Apostolic Leader, Prophet and Pastor
Group Senior Pastor at New Life Restoration Group of Churches International

Foreword

I absolutely love preaching the Gospel. It is truly one of the greatest joys and privileges of my life.

Unfortunately, like so many Christian words, some of the impact of the word "Gospel" has been lost due to it becoming another religious term we use. But the Gospel literally means GOOD NEWS! We're so religious sometimes that even when we say, "good news," it has a religious tone. But it really is the amazing, beautiful, life-changing news that Jesus is alive, He loves us, He died for our sins so that we could have our sins completely forgiven and that we could be completely restored in an intimate relationship with Him. And that is what it really is all about. He loves us and wants to be with us!

When I gave my life to Jesus, I had a powerful encounter with His tangible love that enveloped my whole body, and the next day I woke up a brand-new person. I felt light, free, clean, and I felt like I could fly. I was truly born again! It was so glorious. Later that day, I was baptized with the Holy Spirit and had another power-filled encounter. This all happened at a Christian camp in the Bay of Islands in New Zealand, and I truly was transformed.

But that was only the very beginning of my walk with Jesus. My ongoing transformation, growth, and maturing will surely last the rest of my life. Thirty-four years later, I am still walking with Jesus, and I thank God that I am not the same person I was at fifteen. Together we have been through many great battles and won great victories. Many high highs and many low lows. Mountaintops and valleys—and I've had so many incredible adventures with Him on every continent (except Antarctica!). I've grown a lot in all these years as the Lord has beautifully disciplined, corrected, stretched, challenged, and "shepherded" me so well. But here's the thing ... I've still got miles to go, and miles to grow.

This is the Christian life: one of continual growth, stretching, sanctification, discipling, and maturing. And along the way, a lot of obedience, messing up, repentance, and grace... with the goal that the "messing up" part happens less and less as the Lord continually refines us, shapes us, and moulds us into who He truly created us to be.

Even in the life of Jesus, He *"increased in wisdom and stature, and in favor with God and men."* (Luke 2:52)

He is the author and perfecter of our faith (Hebrews 12:2), and even then, Jesus does this in partnership and agreement with ourselves—our continual surrender, our continual choosing Jesus, to put Him first in all things.

The word "disciple," of course, is very close to the word "discipline." The Father disciplines us, and by our own discipline we choose Jesus, and we choose to obey Him.

We choose to make Him Lord. We choose to spend time with Him, read His Word, worship, and preach the Gospel.

This partnership with Jesus is the very process that sees Jesus fully formed in us and we become all who He created us to be. There are no shortcuts to this.

There is a statement that I've made from the pulpit over and over again in the last few years:

"When you give your life to Jesus, you give your life to Jesus."

This is a seemingly obvious and yet profoundly deep truth, and one that bears repeating over and over for all of us. This idea that when we give our lives to Jesus—when we surrender and make Him Lord of our lives—we completely hand over the keys to our life to Him. Not just part of our lives, not just certain areas, certain days, certain seasons or certain times, but our entire lives.

Even though this is true theologically or positionally, it can be much harder to live out. But the Christian life has both a call and essential requirement for it to be lived all the way in—with no compromise, no halfway, both feet in, and completely sold out.

Galatians 2:20 says, *"I have been crucified with Christ! It is no longer I who lives, but Christ who lives in me. And this life that I live in the flesh, I live by faith, in the Son of God, who loves me and gave Himself for me".*

It's literally no longer I who lives, but Christ who lives in me. Wow!

Just as we see in the life and journey of David, when it came time to face the giant Goliath, he didn't suddenly become a giant slayer. He drew on years of being refined by God in the secret place—on the hillside, with the sheep, when no one was watching. David was prepared by a life of obedience, surrender and trust.

"Your servant used to keep his father's sheep, and when a lion or a bear came and took a lamb out of the flock, I went out after it and struck it... The Lord, who delivered me from the paw of the lion and from the paw of the bear, He will deliver me from the hand of this Philistine." (1 Samuel 17:34–37)

God had been preparing David all along. The battles he fought in private were shaping him into the man who would one day take down a giant in full view of a nation. That's the journey of sanctification.

And that's exactly why I love this book, Gilgal to Bethel. Nico Smit has written a timely, clear, and powerfully prophetic call to us all—not just to be saved, but to become ALL that we were created to be. Not just to get out of Egypt, but to actually go in and possess the land God has promised us.

This book isn't just theory—it's fire. A practical road map if you will, for walking the road of sanctification, transformation, and maturity. Nico doesn't just talk about going deeper—he lays out how. Page after page, chapter after chapter, he points us forward, calling us out of spiritual survival, where so many live, and into what I like to call "thrival". Living in fullness.

If you're hungry for more—then don't just read this book. Let it read you. Let it challenge you. Let it provoke you to move again. This is a book that reminds us we weren't just saved from something... we were saved for something.

So, it's my great privilege to recommend this book to you. Not as a nice devotional, but as a prophetic manual for the road ahead. Let's go from Gilgal to Bethel—and beyond.

>Ben Hughes, Dallas TX, USA
>*Revivalist, Author, TV Host, Pastor and International Speaker*
>*Founder and president at Pour It Out Ministries*
>*Author of "When God Breaks In: Secrets to a Lifestyle of Tangible Encounters with God"*

Introduction: The Journey Beyond Salvation

Will you come into all that God has prepared for you?

Our life with God begins at salvation. It is not meant to be a mere state of existence or a final destination, but the beginning of a new relationship, an amazing adventure and a journey with God that grows fuller and richer with every passing day. It is not a one-sided thing. We get to do it with God, in God and by God.

Nobody has ever had more of God by giving Him less. From the outset, I want you to understand that life with God must be active and intentional. He doesn't ask us to drift through the days or sit in spiritual limbo. The call to holiness flows from our love for Him and His love for us. God encourages us to draw close, inviting us to walk with Him daily. To live with purpose, move in promise, and to experience the richness of life shaped by His presence.

The message of *Gilgal to Bethel* is a prophetic summons to rise from the wilderness of just surviving, and to step fully into the promised land of transformation. It is a divine nudge to those who have been saved from Egypt but are not yet walking in Canaan. To those who have enough faith to be delivered, but not yet enough to be established. This is the cry of heaven: "Come further."

God did not bring you out of your past to leave you halfway to His promises. He did not deliver you simply to abandon you running in circles. He did not send Jesus to just rescue you, but to raise you into His likeness.

This is sanctification - the ongoing process of becoming who you were redeemed to be!

The New Testament never calls believers "sinners saved by grace", but saints – *hagioi* – those who are *being made* holy. Sanctification is essential. It is the whole point of salvation. God saves, but He also sanctifies. And we, by the Spirit, partner in this glorious, gritty, transformative process.

Sanctification is a continual surrender. A lifelong partnership with Holy Spirit. A daily choice to yield our hearts, renew our minds, crucify our flesh, and follow Jesus wherever He leads. As Romans 12 verse 1 says, we are to offer our bodies as living sacrifices, holy and pleasing to God. That means this journey requires intentionality, movement, and faith.

You will not drift into holiness. Nobody will ever stumble into purity. No one ever wakes up accidentally transformed. There is no coasting into maturity. That is why this book is about *daily advance*. We are called to press in, to move forward. Always forward, deeper into grace. Higher in vision. Stronger in faith. Bolder in obedience. Hungrier for righteousness.

The Israelites' journey from Egypt to the Promised Land is a prophetic map for the believer's sanctification. And while it took them forty years of wandering and seven more years of conquest to take what God had already promised, it should never have taken that long. What could have been a two-week journey became a generational delay. And so it is with many today. We cry out for freedom, but resist the formation required for fullness. We long for the fruit of the land but drag our feet when God calls us to walk by faith into it. Like Israel, we often find ourselves caught between what we've been rescued from, and what we have yet to fully enter.

We are called out, but not yet walking in. We are rescued, but still circling around the same old struggles. The open door lies before us. The promise is secure, but the land must be possessed.

The goal is not just to come out of Egypt. It is to go into Canaan.

Jesus said, *"I came that you may have life, and have it more abundantly."* (John 10:10) He was not speaking only of eternal life. He was describing a fullness, a richness, a depth of life in the here and now, a life that overflows with righteousness, peace, and joy in the Holy Spirit.

Yet too many settle for less. They cling to manna when God is offering milk and honey. They remain comfortable in wilderness habits. But wilderness is not your inheritance. It is not your destiny. It is only supposed to be your transition.

Salvation got you out of Egypt. Mercy carried you through the wilderness. But it is a life surrendered that will bring you into the Promised Land!

The call to sanctification is a loving invitation. Don't ever think of it as a burden. God is not demanding performance. He is offering partnership. He wants to do life *with you*, not just *for you*. He wants to live in you, move through you, abide with you.

Your ashes for beauty. Your weakness for His strength. Your sin for His righteousness. Your barrenness for His abundance. This is what the process of sanctification is all about. We must trade what we have for something immeasurably better. The road to more always travels through surrender.

Jesus spoke much about sanctification. He did not simply call people to be forgiven. He called them to be transformed. *"Go and sin no more."* (John 8:11). Not because He expected perfection by our own strength, but because He offers power by His Spirit. Grace is the power to become free, not the excuse to continue to live a life of sin.

This is what it means to walk the path from Gilgal to Bethel.

Gilgal was the place of cutting, the rolling away of Egypt's shame. Bethel was the place of habitation, the house of God, the dwelling of His presence. What lies between is the land of sanctification. It is the walk. The transformation. The contending. The obedience. The yielding.

From beginning to end, it is about being changed. From carnal to spiritual, from survival to fruitfulness, from miracle to blessing, God will not leave us unchanged. Our part hangs on our willingness to submit to His holy process.

Many believers today are still living on manna, mistaking the provision of grace for the fullness of promise. A miracle is God's visit in your life, a blessing is His habitation.

God's desire has never been to merely visit His people with emergency supply. He wants sons and daughters to live in the continual overflow of His goodness. While the world scrambles from crisis to crisis, looking for the next breakthrough, the children of God are invited to live in a perpetual inheritance of love, provision, health, peace, and divine alignment.

A miracle is a financial windfall; a blessing is prosperous living. A miracle is healing; a blessing is walking in divine health.

We must shift from survival to occupation of the land we live in. From depending on manna to cultivating vineyards in the land of blessing. The wilderness was a place of daily miracles, but Canaan is the land of *permanent habitation*, where heaven's flow doesn't fall from the sky, it rises from within.

What Sanctification Actually Looks Like

Sanctification can sound intimidating or theological, but it is intensely practical. To journey down the path of sanctification, we must continually make the small but significant choices that lead us into communion with God. It looks like:

- Praying when it's easier to scroll.
- Choosing integrity when no one is watching.
- Refusing bitterness when you could be justified.
- Worshiping when your soul feels dry.
- Saying "yes" to God again, even after a hard day.

It is your "yes" in the quiet place. It is your "no" when sin whispers its temptation. It's your continual turning toward the face of Jesus. Surrender is our choice to believe God long before we ever run out of other options.

Sanctification is not performance; it is proximity. The closer you draw to Him, the more your life changes. Holiness is a byproduct of that intimacy with the Lord.

God Is Ready—Are You?

We are living in a moment of divine urgency. The Holy Spirit is stirring hearts with a prophetic call: *"It's time to move. It's time to rise. It's time to live in the land I've prepared for you."*

This is not the season for coasting. This is not the time to sit still and admire promises from a distance. God is preparing a sanctified people to inhabit the fullness of what Jesus purchased. This is the year of the SUPERNATURAL! Be assured, though, this road to fullness only travels through a surrendered life.

There is a call going out across the Body of Christ: *"Sanctify yourselves, for tomorrow the Lord will do wonders among you!"* (Joshua 3:5). Heaven is not waiting on another sermon, another conference, or another revival tent, it's waiting on a sanctified people to cross over.

Jesus: The Model of Sanctified Living

Jesus *showed us* what sanctified living looks like. He lived in intimacy with the Father, walked in obedience, and modeled purity under pressure. Every word He spoke was aligned with heaven. Every act He took reflected the will of the Father. Even in the wilderness, He didn't crumble; He overcame.

He lived the blessed life. Throughout His life, Jesus walked under an open heaven, except for one moment; when He took on sin. That's what broke communion with His Father.

Jesus is our example. He didn't survive on manna. He walked in favor. And He invites us to do the same: to abide, to obey, to overcome. Sanctification is not merely about avoiding sin, it's about becoming like Christ. It is Christ in you, the hope of glory (Colossians 1:27).

This book is an invitation to leave behind the wilderness of survival Christianity and enter the house of God, the place of promise. It is a call to abandon the "manna mentality" that lives from moment to moment, barely holding on, and embrace instead a life of overflow. Not by striving, but by surrendering. Not by performance, but by presence. Not by earning, but by abiding.

The land has already been given. The promises already spoken. The blessings already secured in Christ. But you must set your foot there. You must advance. You must go from where you are to where He is calling you.

"You've dwelt long enough at this mountain. Turn and take your journey... See, I have set the land before you; go in and possess it." (Deuteronomy 1:6-8).

God is calling you out of stagnation and into sanctification. He is calling you out of survival and into surrender. He is calling you out of passivity and into possession.

Will it be easy? No. There will be giants. But since when do giants determine God's will?

God is saying, *"I want more than manna for you."*

God wants your whole heart. And He has already given you everything you need to do just that. His Spirit, His Word, and His Presence.

The same Spirit that raised Jesus from the dead lives in you (Romans 8:11). The power to overcome sin lives in you. The capacity to walk in holiness lives in you. The grace to transform is alive in you.

This book is a prophetic guide into the daily advancement of a holy life, not for the sake of religion, but for the sake of relationship. It is the journey of knowing God deeper, seeing Jesus more clearly, and walking in step with the Holy Spirit every single day.

From Gilgal to Bethel. From consecration to habitation. From wilderness to wonder.

And if you're wondering if there is more to this life of faith than you've experienced so far, let me be the one to tell you: there is.

There is so much more!

Jesus didn't live and die and live again, just to get you to heaven. He did it all to get heaven into you. To bring you into fullness, to bless you, to inhabit you, and to make you holy for this life. Your life and how you live it right now matters for eternity!

Let the journey begin! It's time to walk the road of surrender.

1

Salvation Is Out Of Egypt—Sanctification

Most believers know what it's like to cry out to God in desperation and receive deliverance. That moment of salvation is powerful, miraculous, and foundational.

But salvation was never meant to be the finish line; it's only the beginning. Salvation gets you out of Egypt, but sanctification gets you into Canaan. And there's a world of difference between the two.

The Israelites' journey from Egypt to the Promised Land is a prophetic map that helps us consider what sanctification can look like. A key difference being the reality that it shouldn't take us as long as it did for them.

> WHAT COULD HAVE BEEN A TWO-WEEK JOURNEY, BECAME A GENERATIONAL DELAY.

And so it is with many today. Salvation gets you out, but sanctification takes you in.

Out of Egypt... But Into What?

God saved Israel not merely to free them from Pharaoh's grip, but to lead them into a land of abundance, a place flowing with inheritance, blessing, and fruitfulness. He called them to a territory where heaven and earth intersect, where sons walk in favor and provision, where every step forward becomes a declaration of faith.

That sacred ground had already been promised. Yet, many departed Egypt only to fall short of the promise. They cried for liberation but resisted transformation. They celebrated deliverance while shrinking back from the fire that purifies. Rather than stepping into dominion, they remained content in survival.

They had enough faith to leave Egypt, but not enough to occupy the Promised Land.

The crowd in Jerusalem welcomed a Savior, but never yielded to a Lord. They embraced a Deliverer, but not a Sanctifier. Their mouths shouted "Hosanna," but their hearts failed to follow the cloud. As a result, they circled a wilderness for four decades, watching the same terrain, facing the same fears, repeating the same delays, and wondering when breakthrough would finally arrive.

The journey was intended to lead them straight into fullness. Yet, they continued to live on yesterday's grace, blind to the invitation that stood before them daily. Many refused the discomfort required to grow. Though their chains had fallen, their inner world remained unchanged. Egypt still echoed in their appetites, their attitudes, and their unbelief.

What had been promised remained untouched—not due to God's limitation, but because of hearts unwilling to walk forward. The wilderness revealed more than just direction; it exposed desire. And their desire stopped short of transformation.

> THEY WERE OUT OF EGYPT, BUT EGYPT WAS NOT YET OUT OF THEM.

There was provision in the desert, but the land held promise. There was covering, but not cultivation. There was movement, but no maturity. It became a holding pattern, not a habitation. Yet the call from heaven remained constant: move in, possess, inhabit, multiply.

God didn't bring you out to abandon you halfway. He never intended for His people to stay in transition. Mercy provided manna. Love covered failure. But the invitation always pointed forward. Not toward endless wandering, but into promise. Not toward performance, but habitation. Not toward survival, but transformation.

Deuteronomy 1:6–8 captures the moment: *"You have dwelt long enough at this mountain. Turn and take your journey... See, I have set the land before you; go in and possess it."*

So many today remain camped at a spiritual mountain God has already moved on from. The invitation stands wide open, yet the tents of familiarity hold them hostage. The same routines, the same language, the same limits—the land ahead remains unclaimed.

I ask you this: What's the point of salvation if you won't walk into your promised land?

Sanctification is the next step. It brings transformation from glory to glory. It moves the believer from deliverance to dominion, from encounter to establishment. The blood of Jesus opened the door; His Spirit calls us to walk through it.

Every promise from God comes with an invitation to rise, to trust, and to occupy. The question is not whether you're free from Pharaoh. The question is whether you will follow the Presence into the place He prepared.

The Manna Mentality

God graciously provided for the Israelites even in the wilderness. Manna fell daily, water flowed from rocks, a cloud covered their days and a pillar of fire protected their nights. But none of that was His end goal. Manna was a mercy, a temporary provision. Manna was grace for the homeless. It was provisional, temporary, and conditional. It was incomplete.

It's no small miracle to wake up each morning to supernatural food.

But even miracles can become a limitation if we treat them as destinations.

> MANNA SUSTAINED THEM, BUT IT WAS NEVER MEANT TO SATISFY THEM.

God was not content, because this is not ultimately what He wanted or prepared for them.

The danger of the manna mindset is that it allows us to camp in survival instead of pressing into blessing. It causes us to settle for "What is it?" (the meaning of the word manna) when God is calling us into "This is it!"

Faith That Follows

Faith isn't just for leaving the past, it's for following God into the unknown. The people of Israel had faith to cry out for deliverance, but when they reached the borders of the land, their hearts failed them. They feared the giants more than they trusted the God who had already parted seas.

Faith to leave must become faith to follow. Jesus forms us. He rescues us *from* sin and transforms us *into* His likeness. As 1 Corinthians 1:30 says: *"You are in Christ Jesus, who became to us wisdom from God, righteousness and sanctification and redemption."*

Sanctification is a process that requires faith, obedience, and a heart that longs to live in the land God has prepared.

When the Manna Ceased

There came a day when God stopped the manna. Not because He abandoned His people, but because He was calling them higher. Joshua 5:12 tells us: *"The manna ceased on the day after they had eaten of the produce of the land… and the children of Israel no longer had manna."*

That day marked a shift from God's handouts to God's harvest. From dependence to dominion. From wandering to possessing. It was the day they began to eat the food of Canaan, the food they had to cultivate, sow, and reap.

> HE WAS GIFTING THEM LAND,
> NOT A PACKED LUNCH.

God wants more than a manna packed lunch for you too!

The end of manna was also an invitation to maturity. The cloud had lifted, the pillar of fire had stopped moving, and now they had to follow the Ark, God's manifest presence.

God was calling them closer. More personal. It was also God's encouragement to grow up!

There is a point in every believer's journey when the question becomes:

Will you stay in survival or move into sonship?

Sons don't just eat at the door—they live in the house.

They don't beg for crumbs—they prepare feasts.

They don't wait for daily miracles—they build with heaven's blessing.

Jesus Saves—Holy Spirit Sanctifies

There's a reason Scripture refers to believers as saints, *hagioi*, those being made holy. Sanctification is not optional. It's not advanced Christianity. It is the Christian life. Life after salvation is a continual and mighty process of sanctification.

God saves, but it is the believer's responsibility to cooperate with Holy Spirit daily in His work of destroying anything that would keep the believer from enjoying the fullness of the life Jesus brought them into.

We must surrender daily, die to self continually, and keep the fire on the altar burning. Holy Spirit doesn't sanctify us against our will. He waits for our invitation, for our yieldedness, for our yes.

The Difference Between Leaving and Living

Let's be honest; many Christians have left Egypt, but they still live like slaves. They're free but not fruitful. Saved but not sanctified. Forgiven but not filled. They're still camped in the wilderness, wondering why they haven't seen the promises.

Here's why: The Promised Land doesn't come to you. You have to go to it!

God says He will give you every place on which the sole of your foot treads. Unless you set your foot on something new, there is nothing more for God to give you.

> FAITH WALKS. FAITH MOVES FORWARD.

Faith steps out even when the land is still occupied. God told Israel He had given them the land, but they had to possess it. That meant giants had to be driven out, strongholds had to be torn down, and the people had to take responsibility for what had been entrusted to them.

From What Is It... To This Is It!

The Hebrew word *manna* literally means: *What is it?* It was named after confusion. After mystery. After a question.

How many believers today are still living in the "What is it?" season of their faith—confused, waiting, circling, surviving. But God wants to move His people into the "This is it!" season. The season of answered promises. The season of harvest. The season of sonship.

Wilderness was good, Promised Land was better, but Kingdom is best. Jesus came to bring us into God's Kingdom.

Why live on what falls from the sky when God is calling you to plant, water, and reap? Why live in "barely enough" when you're called to "more than enough"? Why beg for breakthrough, when you're called to build in blessing?

Breaking the Manna Mentality

A *manna mentality* is not empowering. It keeps people dependent, afraid to risk, afraid to sow, afraid to trust God with more. A *manna mentality* makes people act entitled, making demands rather than seeing God's wonderful opportunities. It makes Christianity about waiting for God to show up, instead of realizing that He already has. Manna speaks about survival. God talks about abundance.

The only way to break the manna mindset is to start living like someone who has moved into Canaan. That means:

- Trusting God to bless your hands, not just feed your mouth.
- Sowing seed, not just picking up provision.
- Fighting for territory, not just praying for mercy.

It's time to start living as a child of God. The Promised Land of the Old Testament is a picture of the abundant life Jesus speaks of in John 10:10: *"I came that they may have life, and that they may have it more abundantly."*

Canaan is not heaven; it's the Kingdom life available to every believer here and now. But it must be pursued. Entered. Fought for. Lived in. God won't drive out the giants for you, but He will go with you, help you and give you all you need to do what is needed to fully embrace your full inheritance in Christ.

There's more. But it's *there*, not *here*. God has already said **yes**.
   The only question is: Will you walk it out?

2

The Road To More Is Through Surrender

Every believer will eventually come to a crossroads in their journey where the Spirit of God invites them to step further into the fullness of life in Christ. That intersection always demands surrender. The way forward is not through effort, performance, or striving. It is through surrender. The more a believer yields, the more the life of God flows. Surrender is the key that opens what self-protection blocks. It creates the capacity for divine fullness to fill every space previously held by fear, pride, or self-reliance.

> SURRENDER IS NOT WEAKNESS.

It is not giving up. It is not passivity or spiritual laziness. It is a conscious, consistent yielding of one's life to the authority, presence, and leadership of God. True surrender is not a feeling. It is not emotional collapse. It is a faith-filled decision to live laid down. When Scripture calls for a living sacrifice, it is describing the heart posture of one who daily presents their body, mind, desires, and decisions on the altar of God's higher purposes The problem with living sacrifices is they can crawl off the altar. And many do.

Many sing about surrender while maintaining control. They talk about yielding while setting the terms of their obedience. This selective submission reveals an underlying mistrust. They want the benefits of God without the boundary of His Lordship. But God cannot fill what is partially withheld. He will not anoint what is still owned by self. He blesses what is brought to Him fully.

The road to more is paved with surrender. It is the narrow way Jesus spoke of. It is the cross-shaped path of those who have died to self and live unto righteousness.

The beauty of surrender is not just in what it costs, but in what it produces. The life yielded becomes a conduit for heaven. The heart laid bare becomes fertile soil for fruitfulness. There are levels of intimacy, power, and freedom that only open through deeper surrender. What many call supernatural, Scripture presents as the natural outworking of a fully yielded life. The early church did not walk in power because they had better meetings. They walked in power because nothing was off-limits for God. Their time, their finances, their families, their futures—all of it belonged to the Lord.

Surrender begins where our strength ends. As long as we maintain backup plans, we should not be surprised when our spiritual life remains stagnant. Surrender is when there is no plan B. It is the place where God is no longer invited as a consultant, but enthroned as King. Many want a divine helper. Few enthrone a divine Master. God responds to altars, not negotiations. He moves with fire where there is sacrifice. His presence dwells where there is no resistance. Many visit God like a weekend guest. But He does not want visiting rights. He wants habitation.

> HE WANTS TO MOVE IN, NOT BE SCHEDULED IN.

That kind of dwelling demands space. And space is made through surrender.

There is a reason Romans 12 begins with the command to offer our bodies as living sacrifices. Everything else flows from that act. Transformation does not come by willpower. It flows from yieldedness. Renewal of the mind follows offering of the body. Discernment of God's will follows surrender of self-will. Yet many try to skip to spiritual clarity while clinging to personal autonomy. It does not work. God is not mocked. We reap what we sow. If we sow control, we reap confusion. If we sow surrender, we reap revelation. Many are asking God for direction while ignoring His first instruction: lay it all down.

The difference between true surrender and spiritual apathy is in expectation. Apathy resigns. Surrender believes. Apathy shrinks back to survive. Surrender advances in trust. Apathy gives up and calls it peace. Surrender lets go and receives power. One is rooted in disappointment. The other is anchored in hope. One disengages. The other leans in. And this is the posture God honors.

God cannot dwell fully in a divided house.

The Holy Spirit is not a roommate. He does not share space with rebellion. He does not tolerate mixing clean and unclean.. He is holy. He sanctifies. He consumes. And the deeper He is allowed to dwell, the more fully we reflect Christ. We are transformed into His image by beholding, by yielding, by surrendering.

The song "I Surrender All" remains one of the most honest tests of spiritual maturity. Many can sing it. Few live it. The word "all" is where the challenge lies. Partial surrender is disobedience. Delayed obedience is also disobedience. What God blesses is the totality of a heart made available to Him. That includes relationships, time, money, opinions, offense, wounds, dreams, gifts, preferences, reputation, and goals. There is nothing that cannot be placed on the altar.

Some hold back thinking God will take what they love. But the truth is, He replaces what is lesser with what is eternal. He exchanges pain for healing. He gives beauty for ashes. He turns fear into power. He transforms brokenness into glory. But that exchange only happens where there is surrender. You cannot hold both your plan and His. You must choose. And that choice opens doors that striving never could.

There is a road that leads to more. More of God's presence. More of His voice. More clarity, fruitfulness, authority, freedom, and joy. But that road does not come through accumulation. It comes through release. It is the downward path to humility that becomes a gateway for the supernatural. It looks foolish to the world. It looks like weakness. But the surrendered life is the most powerful life on earth. It is the life that cannot be shaken. The one who has laid everything down has nothing left to lose. That is the foundation for boldness. That is where courage lives.

> SURRENDER IS NOT A ONE-TIME ACT. IT IS A LIFESTYLE.

It must be revisited daily. The flesh will always attempt to reclaim territory. Pride will disguise itself as wisdom. Selfishness will camouflage itself as discernment. Religion will hide itself as integrity. Control will dress itself as stewardship. But those who live close to the heart of God know when something has crept back onto the throne trying to usurp God's place. They recognize when the fire on the altar has begun to fade. And they return quickly to the place of yielding.

The road to more begins with the question: what am I still holding onto?

Only when everything is on the altar can everything be filled with glory.

This is the journey of sanctification. The moment of salvation delivers us from sin, but surrender brings us into fullness. The Israelites left Egypt through God's might but entered Canaan only through obedience. Their journey reveals that deliverance is the starting point, not the destination. Many are content with escape but resist entry. But God is not looking for wanderers. He is calling for dwellers. He desires a people who live in promise, not those who tour it occasionally. And the only way into that kind of life is the way of surrender.

Surrender is how strongholds fall. It is how healing flows. It is how worship becomes more than a song and prayer becomes more than a monologue. Surrender removes the veil. It invites the fullness of God to fill the temple. Not the one built by hands, but the one built by blood—your very body.

False Surrenders: The Subtle Substitutes

Not all surrender is genuine. In fact, the heart can be deceptive, and many believers walk in what they believe is surrender when it is actually only a shadow of the real thing. False surrender gives the appearance of obedience while preserving control. It uses spiritual language to cover up unresolved resistance. These counterfeit forms of surrender do not fool God, and they do not produce transformation.

Negotiated obedience is one of the most common. It says, "I will obey—as long as I understand the outcome." It demands clarity before commitment. But God rarely shows the entire plan. He speaks in seed form. He tests trust by withholding details. Negotiated obedience reveals a heart that still wants to lead.

Delayed surrender is another form. "I'm going to give it all to God... just not today." This attitude masks rebellion as a process. It looks patient, but it is prideful. It says to God, "I know what You're asking, but I will decide the timing." But God is not waiting for us to feel ready. He is looking for the heart that responds quickly.

Selective surrender is perhaps the most dangerous. It gives God access to parts of the heart while defending others. "You can have my time, but not my finances." "You can use my gift, but not my pain." "You can call me to serve, but not to forgive." Partial surrender is full disobedience. God does not dwell in divided houses.

Then there is *religious surrender*. This is outward compliance without inward agreement. It sounds spiritual. It checks boxes. It raises hands and sings loudly. But beneath the surface, the heart remains untouched. Religious surrender is content with routine but resists the fire that purifies.

None of these lead to transformation. All of them delay the life of fullness God desires to pour out. True surrender holds nothing back. It trusts even when the path is unclear. It responds when God speaks, not when we feel ready. And it gives Him access to every room in the house, not just the guest room.

Biblical Portraits of Surrender

The story of surrender is etched into the lives of every great man or woman used by God. Scripture does not hide their humanity, but it always highlights their yieldedness.

Abraham, standing on Mount Moriah, raising a knife over his only son, is not a picture of a cruel test, but of radical trust. He believed God's character more than he feared the cost. He laid down the promise because he trusted the Promiser.

Mary, visited by an angel with an impossible announcement, responded with quiet courage: "Let it be to me according to Your word." She surrendered her reputation, her body, her future, to become the dwelling place of God. And through her, glory entered the world.

Jesus, sweating blood in a garden, praying through agony, whispers the words that shaped all eternity: "Not My will, but Yours be done." This is surrender in its highest form. A King laying down His crown to carry a cross. Perfect obedience. Perfect trust. Perfect love.

> THESE ARE NOT MYTHS. THESE ARE MIRRORS.

Their stories invite us to live likewise. God still looks for hearts like Abraham's, wombs like Mary's, altars like Gethsemane's. He still chooses surrender as the threshold of glory.

The Warfare of Surrender

Surrender is warfare. Not in the sense of passive resignation, but as a weapon forged in the fire of trust. Every act of surrender weakens the grip of darkness. Every yes to God becomes a no to the enemy. The greatest spiritual breakthroughs often come, not through striving, but through yieldedness.

The enemy's strategy has always been to keep the believer in control. He knows that control limits access. When we cling tightly to our own understanding, our own timeline, our own ways, we leave no room for heaven's power to break in. But surrender dismantles that stronghold. It removes the currency the enemy traffics in—fear, pride, and entitlement.

Scripture says to submit to God, then resist the devil. Not the other way around. Authority flows from alignment. When a life is yielded, heaven backs it. Hell trembles at it. The most dangerous Christian is not the loudest, but the most surrendered. That person cannot be manipulated by fear, distracted by pressure, intimidated by devils or bought by comfort.

Surrender is not waving a white flag to the enemy. It is raising the banner of the King and declaring war on everything lesser. It is saying to God, "You lead, I follow. No terms. No resistance. No retreat." That posture terrifies hell and invites divine acceleration.

The Fruit of a Surrendered Life

A surrendered life does not stay barren. It becomes fruitful. What begins with letting go ends with overflow. The heart that fully yields to God becomes a channel for heaven's abundance.

Peace begins to reign, not circumstantial peace, but a deep, immovable shalom that anchors the soul even in stormy waters. Joy returns: not surface happiness, but joy rooted in union with God. Discernment sharpens. Clarity increases. Confusion lifts.

Relationships begin to align. Hidden wounds receive healing. The voice of God becomes more familiar, more tender, more compelling. Decisions become less about reaction and more about revelation.

Surrender also produces authority. Those who yield most deeply to God carry the weight of His presence with them. They do not need to force doors open. Heaven opens them. Their prayers carry weight. Their words carry life. Their walk carries peace.

And above all, a surrendered life reveals Christ. It shines with a purity that cannot be manufactured. It breathes with a love that cannot be imitated. It reflects the beauty of a life no longer its own.

Surrender as a Daily Practice

Surrender must become a rhythm, not a reaction. It is not a moment locked in memory. It is a habit, a posture, a way of living. Each day carries fresh opportunities to lay down control and trust God more deeply.

Practicing surrender means asking daily questions: Where am I resisting God? What part of my heart have I reclaimed? Is there an area I once yielded that I have since pulled back? Am I still tender when He speaks?

It also means creating space, moments of silence where the soul listens, places of honesty where confession is welcomed, decisions made not from pressure, but from peace.

Surrender doesn't begin in crisis. It begins in choice. Before the storm hits, the heart is already positioned. Before the battle begins, the sword has already been laid down. And that kind of preparation protects peace in the heat of spiritual warfare.

Those who practice surrender learn to live light. They travel without the weight of self-will. They move with the cloud. They stay ready for God's next move, because they have no need to defend their own plan.

Kingdom Habitation vs. Occasional Visitation

There is a difference between those who visit God's presence and those who live there. Many believers know what it means to encounter God in powerful moments, but few have built a life where He stays. God does not long for an appointment. He longs for a home.

Habitation requires space. It demands holiness. It asks for full access. God fills what is made available. If He is only given Sunday mornings or crisis moments, then only a sliver of His presence can dwell. But when the whole life is open, the whole Kingdom begins to manifest.

The shift from visitation to habitation comes through surrender. When God no longer needs an invitation because He has a residence, the atmosphere of life changes. Worship deepens. Scripture comes alive. Obedience becomes instinctive.

In a house where God dwells, anxiety loses its grip. Confusion is displaced by peace. Sin cannot stay comfortable. Darkness cannot hide. That house becomes a sanctuary, not a performance stage. The difference is not in God's willingness to come, it is in our willingness to yield.

Habitation is what God always wanted. From the garden to the tabernacle to the upper room, His desire has always been to dwell with His people. Not occasionally. Continually. And surrender is the key that turns visitation into permanent residence.

God is searching the earth for those who will yield. Not perform. Not strive. Yield. He is looking for those who tremble at His word, who say yes before they see, who do not flinch when the cost is high. These are the ones who will carry His glory. These are the ones who will see His promises unfold. And their strength will not come from effort, but from surrender.

There is more. But that more cannot be accessed through convenience. The path is narrow. The gate requires letting go. The kingdom belongs to those who become like children, not in ignorance, but in trust. Trust enough to surrender what feels safe. Trust enough to let go of control. Trust enough to believe that what God has in store is worth everything it costs to follow.

> SURRENDER IS NOT LOSS. IT IS THE GREAT EXCHANGE.

Your plans for His purposes. Your anxieties for His peace. Your striving for His rest. Your strength for His Spirit. That is the beauty of the cross. That is the mystery of the kingdom. That is the road that leads to more.

3

The Manna Mentality Must Die

There comes a time in the life of every believer when the provision that once felt like favor, begins to feel like limitation. The grace that once sustained no longer satisfies. The question that arises is not whether God has stopped providing, but whether He is now provoking and inviting His people out of survival and into something greater.

Manna fell from heaven, day after day, for forty years. It was a miracle. A supernatural expression of God's care for a people wandering between bondage and promise. Each morning, they gathered what they needed. They cooked, they ate, they survived. And in that place, God proved His faithfulness.

But manna was never meant to be the food of their destination.

> MANNA WAS NOT MILK AND HONEY.

It was mercy in transition, not the evidence of arrival.

It filled their stomachs, but never filled their purpose. It kept them alive but never taught them how to live. Manna preserved them in the desert, but Canaan was waiting to prosper them in the land.

Manna was grace, but it was not the goal. It was provision, not promise. It came without sowing, without reaping, without building, without ownership. It required no discipline, no risk, no partnership. And that's what made it dangerous. It kept them dependent, but not devoted. Fed, but not fruitful.

Many believers today still live under the influence of the manna mentality. It shows up in their expectations, their prayers, their theology. They pray for God to drop solutions from the sky rather than asking Him to teach their hands to plant and harvest. They wait for deliverance when God has already issued marching orders. They mistake provision for approval, and survival for blessing.

> THE MANNA MENTALITY RESISTS RESPONSIBILITY.

It is shaped by the wilderness, not by the promise. It has been trained to expect God to show up at the door, solve every crisis, and ask for nothing in return. It celebrates miracles but avoids maturity. It sings about freedom but refuses formation.

Manna is for the homeless. It's grace for the wandering. It is divine compassion when roots have not yet been planted. But it was never meant to raise sons. It cannot carry the weight of inheritance. You cannot rule a land on handouts. A slave may be sustained by daily bread, but a son is called to build the family estate.

When Israel crossed into Canaan, the manna stopped. The heavens didn't close. God didn't grow silent. But the season shifted. The miracle ceased, and the harvest began. They ate of the fruit of the land.

They dug wells and drank from them. They planted, built, and multiplied. For the first time, they lived, not just breathed.

The ending of manna was not punishment. It was permission. It was God saying, "Now you are ready."

> IT WAS HIS WAY OF MOVING THEM FROM DEPENDENCE INTO DOMINION.

The stopping of the miracle was the start of maturity. And only those willing to shift their mindset could thrive in the new season.

The manna mentality must die in order for the Canaan mindset to rise. The believer must learn to stop asking, "Where is the miracle?" and begin to declare, "Where is the land I must cultivate?" We are not called to live by daily desperation but by daily partnership with God. Not by emergency prayers but in abiding presence.

Thriving in the kingdom requires a transformation of identity. Slaves beg for crumbs. Sons receive keys. Slaves ask if there will be enough. Sons learn to multiply what they've been given. Slaves live for the moment. Sons prepare for generations. The Father's heart is not for His children to survive—His desire is that they flourish.

To continue asking for manna when the Promised Land lies open, is to dishonor what God has already provided. The wilderness was never meant to define the believer. It was the classroom, not the calling. It was the in-between, not the inheritance. Those who choose to stay in that space when the invitation to enter has been given, are not waiting on God—He is waiting on them.

Living from needing one miracle after another may seem spiritual. It may feel like faith. But in many cases, it's actually avoidance. A continual dependence on supernatural rescue can reveal a refusal to take responsibility for the blessing already made available. Maturity does not reject miracles—it builds a life where miracles are no longer emergencies, but celebrations. A life where miracles are surprising gifts flowing out of God's kindness not our desperation for them.

Canaan is not the absence of God's provision. It's the fullness of it. It is the place where His blessing flows through the work of your hands. Where wisdom, strategy, and stewardship become channels of grace. Where the daily bread doesn't fall from the sky but grows in the fields you've cultivated with Him.

The moment Israel set foot in the land and tasted its fruit, the season of manna closed. Not because God changed, but because His people did. They had stepped into identity.

> THEY HAD CROSSED THE LINE FROM BEING KEPT ALIVE TO BEING CALLED TO BUILD.

The kingdom was never meant to be inhabited by beggars. The Father prepares a table, not a take-out window. His children are not called to visit His goodness, they are meant to dwell in it. Dependency on crisis miracles can feel spiritual, but they often reveal that the heart has not yet learned to rest in blessing.

The mind that has been shaped by scarcity, fear, and constant emergency must be renewed. Otherwise, when blessing comes, it will be mismanaged or rejected. The person who only knows how to survive will not recognize how to steward peace. When manna is no longer available, the insecure heart wonders if God has abandoned them, when in reality He has trusted them with more.

This is the moment where faith must mature. Where the child who cried out for rescue becomes the builder who carries His glory. Where provision becomes partnership. Where surviving gives way to thriving.

Where the question is no longer, "Will God provide?" but "How will I build with what He has given?"

The manna mentality can feel safe. It removes risk. It delays responsibility. But it also prevents growth. If manna keeps falling, there is no need to plant. If water keeps flowing from rocks, there is no reason to dig wells. If the fire keeps leading, there is no need to discern. But sons are called to build altars for intentional worship, not merely rely on pillars or clouds. They are called to follow the Spirit, not just the signs.

God is not raising a people who wait on crumbs. He is raising sons and daughters who walk in wisdom, authority, and abundance. Sons and daughters who understand that the wilderness was mercy, but the land is their mandate. That miracles were proof of love, but blessing is proof of partnership.

Spiritual Dependency vs. Kingdom Maturity

There is a difference between dependence on God and immaturity in the Spirit. Scripture calls us to abide, to trust, to rely fully on the Lord, but not to remain in spiritual infancy. A child cries for every need to be met externally.

> A MATURE SON WALKS IN ALIGNMENT, STEWARDSHIP, AND RESPONSIBILITY.

The manna mentality confuses emotional dependence with spiritual trust. It expects God to do everything while avoiding the process of growth. But Kingdom maturity is not self-reliance, it is Spirit-formed resilience. It doesn't replace grace with striving; it partners with grace to produce fruit.

God wants to walk with you, not carry you forever. He desires intimacy, not codependence. The shift from manna to maturity means moving from a lifestyle of needing rescue to one of ruling with wisdom and grace. It is no longer "God, do it for me," but "God, do it through me."

The way God provides is often a test of what we believe. The wilderness revealed what lived in the hearts of the people. Manna came with instructions; take only what you need for the day, trust Him for tomorrow, don't hoard, don't manipulate. But even with miracles falling from the sky, hearts filled with fear and rebellion.

Provision can become an idol when it becomes the focus. Many trust *what* God gives more than they trust *who* He is. They measure His goodness by the consistency of external results instead of the constancy of His presence. The manna mentality turns miracles into markers of identity. It bases assurance on what is seen, rather than resting in who God has declared Himself to be.

The test is this: can you follow when there is no sign? Can you believe when the provision changes? Can you trust that God's character is stable, even when the process is not? The person who passes this test is ready to receive not only blessing, but authority.

One of the surest signs that the manna mentality remains is in the way a person speaks. The wilderness trained the people of Israel to complain, question, and assume lack. Even with provision in front of them, they remembered the food of Egypt and called it better. They viewed every inconvenience as abandonment. Their mouths aligned with fear, not faith.

The language of lack must be uprooted. If the mind is renewed but the mouth still curses the season, the fruit will withers. Sons and daughters must learn to speak with the language of possession. They declare what God has said, even when they do not yet see it. They call the land theirs before they taste its fruit. They bless what they're building, even before it's finished.

Heaven responds to agreement. If your words echo wilderness thinking, you will continue to walk in circles. But if your mouth matches God's promise, the atmosphere around you begins to shift.

You can't speak like a slave and expect to reign like a son.

The Glory Is in the Land, Not the Wilderness

God met His people in the wilderness. He showed mercy, revealed His power, and displayed signs. But the cloud and fire were never intended to be the end goal. The tabernacle moved from place to place, but the longing of God's heart was always habitation.

Canaan was the place where God would dwell among His people. Where the ark would find rest. Where worship would rise from permanent altars, not makeshift tents. The wilderness was a mobile encounter. The land was a settled glory.

Remaining in a wilderness mindset limits the expression of God's presence in your life. You might still see moments of power, but the weight of glory is reserved for those who enter in. God is not content with temporary intimacy. He is building a house. He is preparing a people who carry His presence into cities, homes, and nations.

There is a weight of glory that doesn't fall in the wilderness; it only manifests in the land. But first, you must let go of the idea that just enough is enough. Step beyond survival and prepare to host Him fully.

The invitation is open, and the land is in view. The tools are in your hands. But the manna mentality must die. That old way of thinking, that survival lens, must be surrendered. God is not content for you to merely be sustained; He desires that you overflow. The storehouses of heaven are not shut. They're waiting for mature sons to take possession.

You were made for more than maintenance. You were designed for multiplication. The wilderness preserved you. The Father intends to prosper you. But first, the mentality of dependence must give way to the mindset of authority.

So, leave behind the cry for daily crumbs. Set your heart on the harvest. Refuse to live on yesterday's miracle. The land has opened. The manna has ceased. The season has changed. And it is time to build.

4

Gilgal – The Place Of Cutting

There is a point in every believer's journey where the wilderness ends, but the promise has not yet begun. It is a transitional place. Holy ground. A spiritual threshold. Before the people of God could take a single step into their inheritance, they had to stop at Gilgal.

> GILGAL MARKED A DIVINE INTERRUPTION.

A compulsory circumcision. A necessary pause before progress. Though they had left Egypt, crossed the Jordan, and stood on the edges of Canaan, the Lord required one more thing: consecration. God would not let them carry forward what He had already cut away.

Joshua 5 describes it plainly. The first generation had died in the wilderness, and the younger had not yet been circumcised. Though physically free, something still had to be dealt with, something hidden, internal, and deeply symbolic. At Gilgal, the Lord commanded that they be circumcised, renewing the covenant, severing Egypt's residue from their identity.

This act was not about outward religion, but rather inward transformation. They've been removed from Egypt, but in order to change location to the Promised Land, Egypt must also be removed from their hearts. Gilgal became the entry place where the old is rolled away, the shame, the patterns, the mindsets that didn't belong in the land of promise could be cut off, so God's new way could begin.

Many desire the next season without submitting to the cutting off of the current one. But the principle remains: God never calls people into conquest until they've come through consecration. Gilgal is unavoidable for those who want to walk in fullness. It is where the heart is exposed, the flesh is confronted, and obedience is tested.

You cannot cross over carrying what God told you to leave. Some things don't, and should not, go with you into promise. Old loyalties, hidden sins, unresolved wounds, pride, control, self-preservation; these must be cut away.

> GOD LOVES DEEPLY, BUT HE ALSO CUTS DEEPLY.
> Not to wound, but to heal.
> Not to punish, but to prepare.

At Gilgal, the people were camped, vulnerable, and still. There was no rushing through. They could not fight. They could not move. They had to wait until they were healed. The timing of the Lord was precise. Circumcision happened before Jericho. Before victory. Before walls fell. Because God knows that spiritual authority only rests on sanctified vessels.

The cutting at Gilgal also revealed God's patience. He was not in a hurry. The promise waited. The land was not going anywhere. But the people had to be ready. And readiness did not come through momentum, it came through surrender.

Joshua 3:5 captures this posture: "Sanctify yourselves, for tomorrow the Lord will do wonders among you." God's wonders are often withheld, not due to His reluctance but our unreadiness. He is not holding back breakthrough, He is calling for consecration. He is searching for hearts prepared to carry the weight of His glory.

The cutting does not disqualify, it qualifies. Those who submit to God's pruning are the ones He trusts with power. The blade removes what grace never gave. It confronts false identities and kills off spiritual compromise. At Gilgal, the people were marked, not with shame, but with covenant. They emerged not as wanderers but as warriors. The wilderness ended there. A new era had begun.

Gilgal is where the wilderness is buried. Where past mistakes are severed. Where identity is reestablished.

> IT IS THE DIVINE SURGERY
> THAT PRECEDES POSSESSION.

God won't allow mixture in the place of inheritance. He doesn't bring Egypt into Canaan. He brings sanctified sons and daughters.

Crossing the Jordan got their feet wet. But Gilgal cut their hearts open. Both were necessary. One was public. The other, private. There is no entrance into deep promise without private consecration. Public influence without inner cutting becomes corruption. Our flesh will always try to manufacture what can only be birthed through sanctification.

Many resist Gilgal because it feels like delay. But it's actually preparation. It's the love of God removing what would sabotage you later. What He asks to cut now would crush you if carried into the next level. His mercy often comes as a blade. What He cuts, He intends to replace with something greater; clarity, strength, authority, and purity.

There is no shame in being circumcised again. God's people had to go through it even after decades of travel. Because movement is not maturity. The journey does not guarantee formation. There are many who walk long distances spiritually but still carry what needs to be surrendered. Gilgal is the place where years of wandering meet the knife of purpose.

And from that place, the manna stopped. The next day, they ate from the produce of the land. The shift came after the cutting. The supply changed because their identity had changed. They were no longer refugees in waiting. They were a covenant people, healed, marked, and ready.

You cannot bypass the place of cutting. You cannot skip over private surrender and expect to walk in public breakthrough. Gilgal precedes Jericho. Consecration precedes conquest. If you try to shout down walls without submitting your heart, you may stir up noise, but no authority will fall.

Gilgal still calls today. It calls the believer into the hidden place where the Holy Spirit applies the blade. Not out of wrath, but out of mercy. Not to shame, but to purify. It is the Father's invitation to be made ready, to be made whole, to be made new.

The Shame Rolled Away

Joshua 5:9 says, *"Today I have rolled away the reproach of Egypt from you."* That moment at Gilgal wasn't only about cutting the flesh, it was about removing the identity of slavery. Even though they were physically free, shame had followed them. They had crossed a river, but Egypt still echoed in their thinking.

Shame is a subtle tormentor. It whispers that you'll always be who you were. It lingers in places of past failure. But Gilgal marks the moment when the name of shame is rolled away. God doesn't just forgive sin, He breaks its residue. He removes its mark from your identity.

Many believers walk in forgiveness but still carry a slave mentality. Gilgal says, "No more." God doesn't want sons living under the weight of old labels.

> HE DOESN'T WANT WARRIORS THINKING LIKE WANDERERS.

The cutting is not only for purity, it's for freedom from every lie that said, "You are still who you were in Egypt."

A Hidden Work for a Public War

What happened at Gilgal was private, painful, and deeply personal. No army was watching. No enemy was intimidated. From the outside, Israel looked vulnerable, even foolish. They had crossed into enemy territory and stopped to weaken themselves.

But God is never afraid of appearing weak in the eyes of the world. He does His best work in secret. Gilgal prepared them for Jericho, but no one would have known by looking. The same is true today. The most significant spiritual victories begin in hidden places.

What God does in private sanctifies what He releases in public. If you try to bypass the hidden cutting, your public assignment will crush you. You will have authority without stability. And God loves you too much to promote what He has not purified. The quiet obedience at Gilgal becomes the foundation of confidence on the battlefield.

Consecration Unlocks Clarity

There is a spiritual dullness that lifts when consecration deepens. Many wander in cycles of confusion, asking for revelation without offering surrender. Gilgal recalibrates the heart. It sharpens spiritual hearing. It positions the soul to discern what God is doing.

Before Jericho could fall, Israel had to align. Consecration wasn't a ritual—it was the unlocking of divine perspective. The same happens today. When a believer allows the Spirit to deal with hidden areas, distraction breaks. When the flesh is cut away, the voice of the Lord becomes clearer.

Confusion often clings to divided hearts. A mixture of desire clouds discernment. But when the heart is wholly given, clarity follows. If you can't hear clearly in the present, consider what God may be asking to cut away.

> GILGAL DOES NOT ONLY SANCTIFY THE HEART, IT AWAKENS THE MIND.

The cutting at Gilgal also marked the rise of a new generation. The previous generation had died in the wilderness, but the new one had never been circumcised. This act was more than personal, it was generational. It signified a baton being passed, a mantle being released, a promise re-engaged.

God was raising up a people who would no longer mourn Egypt but would march into promise. The old had walked in circles. The new would walk in conquest. But before they could step into destiny, they had to be marked. This is always the pattern; revival doesn't rest on charisma, but consecration.

Every generation must be cut again. You cannot inherit sanctification from your parents. Every heart must be set apart. Every leader must pass through the blade. The future belongs to those who are willing to be prepared; not in power, but in purity. Gilgal ensures that the next generation does not inherit the wilderness, they inherit the land.

When God calls you to Gilgal, it is not a punishment, it is a promotion. It means you are on the edge of something holy. It means heaven is about to hand you keys. It means the wilderness is over and the land is opening. But it also means you cannot go forward as you have been. What has clung to you in mercy must now be removed in maturity.

Sanctify yourself. Let Him deal with what lies beneath the surface. Yield to the cut. Let go of what never belonged. The next wonder is coming. The land awaits. But first, come to Gilgal, and be made ready.

5

Jericho – The Place Of Obedient Faith

The wilderness had ended. The people had crossed the Jordan. The shame of Egypt had been cut away at Gilgal.

Now, they stood at the threshold of their first battle. Not a spiritual test hidden in the shadows, but a visible, tangible confrontation with the strongholds standing between them and the land of promise. And Jericho towered before them.

Jericho was a symbol. A fortress of resistance. A spiritual wall that dared the people of God to believe their own prophetic future. It represented every barrier, every generational stronghold, every lie that told them they would never make it, never see it, never occupy what God had promised.

Jericho was closed, but it was not locked.

Jericho calls people to choose to see the obstacle or believe what God promised. There was no ambiguity with God. Look at His first words to them, "*See! I have given Jericho into your hand!*" (Joshua 6:2)

Heaven had already decided. Jericho was not a question of *if*—only *how*. And that "how" was going to confront their instincts. The path forward would not be through natural strength, persuasive strategy, or militant power. It would come through obedient faith, the kind of faith that trusts without proof, follows without clarity, and marches without explanation.

God gave Joshua a strange command. March around the walls of Jericho once a day for six days. Do it in silence. Then on the seventh day, circle it seven times, and at the end, let the priests blow their trumpets and the people shout. The walls will fall.

No one had ever fought a battle like this. No swords were drawn. No arrows released. No threats shouted over the ramparts. Just a silent procession of faith circling impossibility.

> THE SILENCE WAS NOT PASSIVE, IT WAS POWERFUL.

It revealed a people who didn't need noise to prove belief. They didn't speak to convince themselves. They didn't argue with the enemy. They didn't need to perform. They trusted. And their trust held its breath.

Obedience, *not volume*, would shake the walls. The silence became worship. Their footsteps became declarations. Their march became warfare. Every lap declared, "We believe God even when nothing moves." And for six days, nothing moved.

This is where many give up. When nothing changes after obedience. When the wall still stands. When the enemy still mocks. But the seventh day always comes. And on that seventh day, something broke. Not because of the volume of the shout, but because of the weight of obedience. Faith had reached its fullness. And the supernatural was released.

> **WALLS FALL WHEN TRUST WALKS.**

Breakthrough happens where obedience is sustained.

Miracles manifest where prophetic instruction is honored.

Too many want to see God move before they obey. But the pattern of Jericho tells us the opposite: you won't see the wall move until you walk. You won't see the atmosphere shift until you keep circling when you feel foolish. You won't see victory until obedience is complete.

What if your breakthrough is waiting on your second lap? Or your sixth? What if the silence is not a sign of failure but the proof of faith?

The Church today is often tempted to shout before obeying. We want to release declarations without embracing discipline. We want warfare without formation. But Jericho shows us that faith is not proved by how loud we shout, it is revealed by how we align our hearts. The people who saw the wall fall were the ones who walked exactly as God instructed. Nothing less. Nothing more.

And that's what makes Jericho prophetic.

It reveals the power of obedient faith in spiritual warfare. Not faith that performs. Not faith that boasts. But faith that follows. Radical trust. Unquestioning obedience. A posture of listening before speaking. Walking before warring.

There is power in prophetic acts. Actions that may look strange to the natural mind but release heaven's authority into the earth. Marching in silence was not strategy, it was surrender. It was God's way of saying, "This victory will not be won by your methods. It will be released through your obedience."

Prophetic acts often precede prophetic manifestation. Throughout Scripture, the pattern is clear. Elijah builds an altar in drought before rain falls. Naaman dips in muddy water before his skin is restored. Jesus spits in the dirt and makes mud to heal a man born blind.

> OBEDIENCE TO UNUSUAL INSTRUCTION
> UNLOCKS UNUSUAL POWER.

Jericho teaches us that spiritual warfare is not always aggressive, it is obedient. Sometimes the loudest shout in the spirit is the quiet consistency of a surrendered heart doing exactly what God said, even when no one understands.

Walls of addiction, fear, unbelief, generational bondage; these often remain, not because God is unwilling to bring them down, but because we haven't yet marched around them with faith that follows all the way through. We talk about the wall. We rebuke the wall. We sing over the wall. But until we walk in obedience, the wall remains.

Obedient faith says, "I don't need evidence to keep moving." It says, "God has spoken—that is enough." It leans into the instruction, no matter how simple or strange. And it keeps walking when logic says to stop.

Jericho is the place where God proves that obedience always precedes victory. Not partial obedience. Not delayed compliance. But full-hearted, step-by-step surrender to divine instruction.

When God gave Joshua the strategy for Jericho, it violated all human reason. March in silence. Circle a city. Blow trumpets. Then shout. No weapons drawn. No ladders scaled. No tactical negotiations. Every part of the instruction required the people to suspend what made sense in favor of what God had spoken.

Obedience rarely feels logical on the front end. It often comes with little explanation, no immediate result, and no confirmation from others. But faith is not agreement with what we understand, it's alignment with what God said. He is not obligated to satisfy our intellect, but He is faithful to fulfil His Word.

What if your next breakthrough depends on following a strange instruction? What if God is asking you to forgive before they apologize, to give when you're in lack, to stay when you want to flee, to serve when you'd rather speak? Faithful obedience often starts with uncomfortable direction.

Jericho reminds us: God doesn't need your strategy; He needs your surrender. When you follow His voice over your logic, the fruit always follows. The wall may not fall on day one, but it will fall. Obedience may not feel productive, but it will be powerful.

> GOD'S INSTRUCTIONS ARE NOT PUZZLES TO SOLVE.
> THEY ARE DOORS TO WALK THROUGH.

Waiting Is Not Wasting

Six days of circling with no visible change. That's what Israel walked through. One lap after another. Morning after morning. The wall still stood. The city still mocked. The atmosphere remained silent. Yet they kept walking.

Most believers struggle not with obedience, but with sustained obedience. It's easy to say yes on day one. It's harder on day four, when nothing has shifted. Many abort the assignment because they confuse stillness with stagnation. But waiting on the Lord is not idleness. It is spiritual alignment. Every lap was preparing their hearts. Every step was building spiritual momentum.

In the kingdom, timing is everything. What feels like delay is often divine positioning. God's process includes quiet days, hidden seasons, and uncelebrated faithfulness. Jericho reminds us: delay is not denial, and waiting is not wasting. Heaven measures obedience not in results but in resolve.

When you keep walking through the silence, something forms in you. Trust deepens. Pride is cut away. Faith matures. And by the time the seventh day arrives, your spirit is ready to release a sound that carries glory. You're not wasting time; you're being made ready.

Obedience is rarely isolated. What Israel did at Jericho was watched by their enemies. The people of Jericho saw the silent march, day after day. And with each lap, fear grew. God was declaring something to the nations through their obedience.

You never walk alone. Your yes to God reverberates beyond your life. Angels take notice. Demons tremble. And people around you begin to feel the atmosphere shift.

> YOUR SURRENDERED OBEDIENCE BECOMES A PROPHETIC WITNESS TO OTHERS WHO ARE WATCHING AND WAITING TO BELIEVE.

When you keep walking in faith, when you stay silent instead of defending yourself, keep showing up instead of quitting, keep giving even when you're not noticed, you are preaching with your life. The sound of your footsteps carries weight in the spirit. God is using your faithfulness to signal His authority.

There are people who will be strengthened by your consistency. People who will find courage to obey because you walked when you didn't see results. Your obedience becomes their confirmation that God is still moving. What you do in quiet trust becomes a prophetic voice that declares, "He is faithful."

The shout on the seventh day wasn't magic. It wasn't a religious tactic. It wasn't hype. That shout carried power because it was built on the foundation of obedience. Every lap, every step, every moment of silence added spiritual weight. By the time the trumpet sounded, the shout was saturated with surrendered faith.

We live in a world obsessed with noise. Volume is mistaken for authority. Performance is confused with presence. But in the kingdom, sound means nothing if obedience is absent. The power is not in how loud you speak, but how deeply you've followed.

You cannot bypass the process and expect to carry the same authority. A shout that follows compromise is just a hollow echo. A declaration that is not rooted in surrender becomes spiritual noise. But when obedience precedes sound, that sound shakes foundations.

When your life is aligned, your voice is sharp. When your walk matches your worship, the atmosphere responds. Jericho fell not because of decibels, but because of devotion. The shout was not the beginning of victory, it was the release of it.

Jericho: The Test of Lordship

Jericho marked the beginning of Israel's campaign in Canaan. It was not chosen at random. Jericho was the first of ten cities in the land, and by divine command, it was to be wholly given to God. Everything in it belonged to Him. Jericho functioned as a tithe; the first portion, the sacred portion. It was to be consecrated, not claimed. Before any inheritance could be enjoyed, God required a demonstration of who truly reigned over Israel.

The instruction to surrender Jericho was a statement of ownership. The land was not theirs until God said it was. The walls could not fall unless God moved. The victory could not be claimed unless God was honored first. This was a Lordship issue. The surrender of Jericho acknowledged that everything beyond it was under divine rule.

Israel had walked in the wilderness for forty years. They had seen miracles. They had eaten manna. But now they were entering a land where they would need to shift from survival to stewardship. And that transition would only be possible if they passed the test of consecration. God demanded Jericho as His own. They could not take it and use it for themselves. No compromise and no shortcuts. Only surrender.

The entire city was to be consecrated. No plunder, no private gain, no exception. The principle was clear: the first belongs to the Lord. To touch what was sacred would be to violate the covenant. And when Achan ignored this command, he brought defeat upon the entire nation. What was withheld from God, God withheld from them.

This pattern remains. The first worship goes to Him. The first decisions go to Him. The first victories are laid at His feet. We do not begin our journey by asserting ourselves. We begin by yielding. The promise can only be occupied if the Lord is enthroned.

Jericho was not a large city. It did not boast the size or population of other strongholds. But it had something that stood in the way; walls. High, thick, impenetrable walls. These walls represented more than military defence. They stood as a visible challenge to the promises of God. Israel could see the land, but this obstacle declared: you shall not pass.

God did not call Israel to scale the wall or shatter it with force. He called them to walk around it. Quietly. Silently. Repeatedly. This made no military sense. But it revealed something deeper. Would they obey without understanding? Would they trust without speaking? Would they follow when it looked foolish? Would they treat this ground as holy?

Before any wall came down, Joshua encountered the Commander of the Lord's army. Sword drawn. Ready. Joshua asked, *"Are you for us or for our adversaries?"* The response cut deep: *"No. But as Commander of the army of the Lord I have now come."* (Joshua 5:13–15)

This answer did not align with Joshua's understanding. The issue was not whether God was for Israel. The issue was whether Israel would submit to God.

> THE COMMANDER DID NOT COME TO ENDORSE A SIDE.
> HE CAME TO RULE.

And in that moment, Joshua fell to the ground face down. The place was holy.

Joshua had a battle plan. But God had a claim. Jericho belonged to Him. The outcome did not depend on Israel's tactics. It depended on their surrender. And the only way forward was downward. God required that Israel start low if they wished to go high. The lowest inhabited city on earth became the place where the highest victory would be initiated.

Jericho was 240 meters below sea level. The lowest city on the planet. Not coincidence, but design. God chose this place to initiate the campaign. The geography was prophetic. The way forward starts from below. The journey into promise begins with Lordship. You will not ascend until you bow.

"My Lord keeps my lamp burning; my God turns my darkness into light. In His strength I can crush an army; with my God I can scale any wall." (Psalm 18:28–29)

The Church today often claims to seek God first, but many begin with ideas and ask for blessing later. Jericho confronts this tendency. It demands that we begin on our faces. Not with our plans, not with our ambition, not with our assumptions. Jericho exposes who truly leads.

Faith was required, but not just any kind. This was a faith that walked in silence, that obeyed when it felt useless, that gave God what was costly. The walls did not fall because Israel was powerful. They fell because the people submitted. And once the walls fell, the entire city was consumed. Not as a show of force, but as an act of worship.

This is why Jericho had to be consecrated. It was an offering. The first belongs to God. All of it. Every stone. Every possession. Every decision. Jericho was not about the enemy's strength. It was about Israel's allegiance.

The enemy was not the greatest challenge. The wall was not the deepest threat. The real test was Lordship. Who owns this land? Who rules this journey? Who commands your heart? Jericho demanded a decision. And so does every believer's entrance into promise.

"The Lord our God said to us at Horeb, 'You have stayed long enough at this mountain. Break camp and advance...'" (Deuteronomy 1:6–8). The mountains were part of the inheritance. But not all of them were yielded in Joshua's day. Joshua failed to fully occupy the high places, and as a result, David would later have to finish the job.

"The king and his men went to Jerusalem against the Jebusites... Nevertheless, David took the stronghold of Zion (that is, the City of David) ... So, David dwelt in the stronghold, and called it the City of David. And he built all

around from the Millo and inward. Then David went on and became great, and the Lord God of hosts was with him." (2 Samuel 5:6–10).

The promise was wide, including plains, valleys, and mountains. But high places were often the last to bow. David understood: you cannot possess all until every high thing is brought low. And when he conquered Jerusalem, he brought in the ark. He enthroned the presence. That's what it looks like to establish sanctification.

Jesus faced the same test. After His baptism and public affirmation, He was led into the wilderness. There, He was tested. *"If you are the Son of God…"* (Matthew 4:1–11). Three temptations. Each one an assault on identity, authority, and worship. But Jesus did what Adam did not. He trusted. He obeyed. He resisted. He stood.

And this is the pattern for us. Every temptation asks: Who are you? Who do you serve? Who do you trust? Who is your Lord?

You cannot see the glory of God fall if Jesus is not seated on the throne of your heart. Give Him your first. Give Him your highest. Let no other name, no other pursuit, no other desire hold sway over you.

We often ask for miracles but withhold surrender. We ask for favor but reserve control. But God does not respond to manipulation. He is not moved by show. He is Lord. He is King. He will have Jericho.

And if we give Him Jericho, everything else will open.

Let Jericho be holy, and let your heart be yielded.

Obedience Trains the Heart for Battle

Jericho was the first of many battles. It was a test, not of military skill, but of trust. Before swords were drawn, before kings were conquered,

God established the foundation: victory would come through obedience.

God wasn't just giving them a city. He was forming a people. He was training them to follow His voice without hesitation, to trust His process without resistance, to move when He said move and be still when He said wait.

The battle wasn't against the wall. The real confrontation was internal. Could they obey without understanding? Could they march without murmuring? Could they follow without proof?

God still trains hearts through obedience. He gives you small assignments to prepare you for larger authority. Every time you obey in hidden places, your spiritual muscles are being strengthened. Every "yes" becomes a weapon.

> EVERY SURRENDER BECOMES A SWORD.

If you want to carry greater spiritual authority, you must first pass through the school of obedience.

Jericho was not a detour, it was preparation for destiny.

When the Strategy Changes, the Standard Stays the Same

Jericho was unique. No other battle in the conquest of Canaan looked like it. Future victories involved ambushes, drawn swords, military plans. God's strategy shifted from city to city. But one thing never changed: His requirement for complete obedience.

The standard remained: hear, trust, follow. Israel could not assume that what worked once would work again. They had to stay in step with the Presence. The formula was not the source of power; obedience was.

Many believers try to replicate what worked in a previous season. They cling to a method, a rhythm, a familiar path. But God is not mechanical. He is relational. He anoints faith.

To walk in victory, you must stay flexible in method but faithful in surrender. Be willing to shift, adapt, and move with the Spirit. When He changes the instruction, the response is still the same: yes, Lord. The standard is trust. The strategy may change, but the requirement never does.

You don't need a better strategy; you need a better yes.

You don't need more volume; you need more trust.

You don't need to convince heaven; you need to align with it.

Faith that walks will always see what faith that hesitates never will.

6

Ai – The Place Of Defeat, Repentance, And Worship

Ai was small. Compared to Jericho, it was insignificant. The spies even told Joshua, "Don't send the whole army; only a few thousand are needed." Confidence was high. Momentum had been building. God had shown His power in undeniable ways. The walls of Jericho had fallen, and the people of Israel were learning to walk in victory. But what came next was unexpected. Defeat.

There is nothing more disorienting than experiencing triumph, only to be met with failure in the next breath. Thirty-six men died at Ai. Panic spread. Hearts crumbled. The people who had marched with confidence now stood in confusion. Joshua fell on his face, asking why. What had gone wrong?

The answer was clear: there had been sin in the camp. Achan had taken what belonged to God and hidden it. He had disobeyed the clear instruction to leave the consecrated things untouched. One man's compromise cost the nation its momentum.

Ai represents the place where hidden sin is exposed. Where what was buried is brought into the light. Where the God who gives victory also demands holiness.

> GRACE DOES NOT EXCUSE COMPROMISE.
> IT INVITES REPENTANCE.

And when repentance is true, restoration is certain.

God takes His presence seriously. He takes His people seriously. What He had begun to build through obedience, He would not allow to be defiled by deception. His love is not permissive; it is purifying. He does not turn a blind eye to sin. He addresses it. Not to shame, but to restore.

There are moments in the believer's journey when God allows defeat, not as punishment, but as a mirror. To reveal what must be dealt with. To expose what is hindering forward movement. Failure, in the hands of God, becomes formation. Ai was not the end. It was a turning point.

Joshua sought the Lord, and the Lord answered.

The issue wasn't strategy; it was sanctity.

The people had violated covenant. And until the offense was addressed, the favor would lift. This is a sobering truth: God will not endorse what He cannot inhabit. He won't put His name on what contradicts His nature.

But even in His correction, there is mercy. God didn't leave Israel in defeat. He instructed Joshua to find the root, to deal with it thoroughly, and to consecrate the people afresh. And when the people responded, when repentance was real, restoration followed.

Hebrews 12:6 says, *"The Lord disciplines those He loves."* Ai reveals that discipline is not rejection. It is redirection. God corrects not to condemn, but to course-correct.

> HE REMOVES WHAT CORRUPTS SO HE CAN RESTORE WHAT WAS LOST.

His heart is not to disqualify but to purify.

Once the issue was dealt with, God gave Joshua a new strategy. This time, they would not fail. In fact, the victory at Ai would be even more complete than Jericho. What began in failure ended in favor. What started with grief ended in glory.

This is the pattern of redemption. When the heart returns, heaven responds. God is not looking for perfection; He is looking for repentance. The power of repentance is that it reopens doors that disobedience shut. It realigns what was misaligned. It clears the path for God to move again.

In every believer's journey, there will be Ai moments. Times when we misstep. Times when we fall. Times when the enemy seems to win. But these moments don't have to define us. They become altars of return. Places where the heart is renewed, the vision is clarified, and the voice of God speaks again.

The danger is not in defeat. The danger is in denial. When we justify compromise, when we excuse disobedience, when we cover what God is trying to uncover, we prolong the wilderness. Ai is meant to be a short chapter, not the whole story. What matters is how we respond.

Repentance is not a one-time event. It is a posture. A heart that stays soft. A willingness to be searched. A readiness to return. Repentance is the doorway to restoration. It is the act of aligning again with truth. Of saying, "God, have all of me, even the parts I've tried to hide."

Achan's sin affected the whole camp. This reveals a critical principle: private compromise has public consequences. What we think is hidden often leaks into the atmosphere around us.

That's why holiness matters.

Not as legalism, but as protection. Not to earn God's favor, but to protect our own hearts and the people around us.

God's presence cannot dwell where rebellion is defended. But when repentance is embraced, His nearness returns. His voice becomes clear. His favor flows again. And the victory that follows will often exceed what we thought we lost.

The second battle at Ai was different. God was with them. Strategy flowed. Confidence returned. And the city fell. This was more than a military win. It was a prophetic declaration: God restores what sin tried to steal.

The shame of failure does not have to be final. Restoration is not only possible; it is promised to the repentant. God delights in bringing beauty from ashes, strength from weakness, hope from the rubble of regret. Ai is not the end. It is a doorway.

In our modern language, we often think repentance is simply saying sorry. But biblical repentance is more than emotion. It is change. It is movement. It is the turning of the heart back to God in full surrender. It is not lip service; it is life realignment.

Many believers want restoration without repentance. They want peace without purity. But God will not bless what He has called us to crucify. Grace is not a hiding place for sin. It is the power to overcome it. Grace strengthens our yes to God and weakens the pull of the flesh.

The message of Ai is this: sin blocks what surrender restores. Obedience opens what disobedience delays.

> THE HANDS THAT HOLD IDOLS
> CANNOT TAKE HOLD OF PROMISE.

But when the idols fall, the gates of blessing open again.

There is something God is willing to give you on the other side of repentance that He will not release in the presence of compromise. Not because He is withholding out of spite, but because He is preserving out of love. Ai was the place where God said, "I want to give you more, but not like this."

The invitation is always open. Return to Me. Let Me deal with what you've buried. Bring it into the light. Trust Me with your exposure, and I will clothe you with righteousness. Let Me purify what has grown polluted. Let Me restore what was taken.

You may have lost a battle, but the war is not over. You may have fallen, but grace is still reaching. The God of Jericho is still the God of Ai. The One who gave victory will give it again, when the heart bows low and the hands open wide.

The Deception of Hidden Things

Achan's sin was not visible on the surface. He had buried what he took beneath his tent; out of sight, but not out of reach. Hidden things are the enemy's playground. What is buried but not brought into the light begins to gain spiritual weight. It attracts confusion, clouds discernment, and weakens authority.

The deception is this: if no one knows, it won't matter. But the kingdom of God functions by a different law. What is covered must be uncovered. What is buried must be surrendered.

> GOD DOESN'T EXPOSE TO EMBARRASS;
> HE EXPOSES TO HEAL.

He reveals in order to redeem.

We cannot carry secret compromise and expect public victory. What is held in the darkness has power over us until it is placed into the light.

The cross does not cover what we refuse to confess. And the Spirit does not anoint what we insist on hiding.

Achan's hidden treasure became a national consequence. Because hidden sin always leaks into and eventually poisons the atmosphere around us. It affects marriages, ministries, families, and faith communities; not through punishment, but through the spiritual breach it creates. Ai reminds us: what we hide is not harmless.

The Holiness of God Demands Alignment

God is not casual about His covenant.

> HE IS HOLY, AND HIS PRESENCE DEMANDS ALIGNMENT,
> NOT APPROXIMATION.

When Israel crossed into Canaan, they stepped into the realm of promise, yes, but also of precision. Every step forward would now require full agreement with God's nature and Word.

At Ai, God withdrew His backing until the breach was addressed. Not because His love was diminished, but because His holiness had been compromised. There are times when the favor of God pauses; not to punish us, but to purify us. It is love that refuses to bless us into destruction. It is mercy that refuses to empower rebellion.

When God lifts His hand, it's not rejection, it's correction. His absence in the moment signals a call to realignment. And when that invitation is honored, the power of God returns in greater force. Holiness is about alignment. It's about giving God every area, not holding any part back.

After the defeat at Ai, Joshua fell before the Lord in grief. He tore his clothes, lay before the ark, and cried out in confusion and sorrow. God met him there, not to coddle him, but to reveal the problem. Sometimes grief is what cracks the heart open enough for God to speak truth.

Spiritual grief, when carried to the feet of God, becomes a gateway to clarity.

It humbles us. It silences our pride. It creates space to hear what we were too confident to listen to before. Joshua's grief became the soil for repentance, the beginning of restoration.

We must learn not to resist grief. It is not the same as despair. Grief has the power to clear the fog. When allowed to run its course in the presence of God, it will always lead us back to alignment. Many want revelation without grief, but the heart must first be tender to hear the truth. Ai teaches us that godly sorrow is a doorway.

The Role of Leadership in Purging Compromise

Joshua did not cause the sin, but as the leader, he was held responsible to address it.

> LEADERSHIP IN THE KINGDOM IS NOT ABOUT POPULARITY, IT IS ABOUT PURITY.

It requires courage to deal with what's wrong, even when it hides in the ranks. Joshua had to go tribe by tribe, family by family, until the breach was found.

True spiritual leadership carries the burden of discernment and discipline. It cannot afford to look away from compromise. It must protect the camp, not preserve comfort. Ai reminds us that leadership will be tested not only in victory but in how it handles defeat.

The purity of the people was tied to the willingness of the leader to pursue holiness. God didn't bypass Joshua but rather He worked through him. And when Joshua obeyed, the camp was cleansed, and victory returned.

Leaders today must reclaim this mantle. We are called to steward the spiritual atmosphere with integrity. Not through public spectacles, religious performances or public opinion, but by sincere pursuits to honor God. Not with shame, but with truth. Not with condemnation, but with clarity. If we want to see lasting breakthrough, we must confront what threatens the presence of God.

Ai was a low point in Israel's story. It exposed weakness, uncovered sin, and brought defeat. But it did not end the journey. In fact, what followed was one of their most decisive victories. The place of failure became a stage for restoration.

God purifies those who respond in meekness. The enemy will always whisper that failure means finality. That if you've lost ground, you've lost the call. But the God of Ai proves otherwise. He doesn't define you by your worst moment but redefines you through repentance.

Failure becomes fertilizer in the life of the surrendered. God builds from broken places. He restores what's been shattered. He rewrites your story. Ai reminds us that restoration is not a return to what was, but a launching into something new.

For anyone who has fallen, for anyone who feels disqualified, Ai declares: if you will repent, you will rise again.

The God Who Confronts Is Also the God Who Commissions

After the sin had been exposed and removed, God didn't just forgive; He spoke again. He gave Joshua fresh strategy, fresh courage, and fresh confidence. God's voice came in strength: *"Do not be afraid. Take the whole army. I have delivered Ai into your hands."*

This is the beauty of divine restoration. God doesn't hold your failure over your head. He doesn't keep you on probation. He speaks again. He calls again. He commissions again. Ai was the site of one of Israel's lowest moments, but it became the soil of their next victory.

God wants to speak again over those who've been silent in shame. He wants to restore prophetic hearing. He wants to give new instruction. The voice that once corrected, now empowers. The same Presence that uncovered sin, now releases victory.

Ai proves that when God finishes dealing with what's wrong, He begins rebuilding what's right. He does not leave the altar cold. He meets it with fire. And He always sends the yielded forward with power.

Ai is the place of confrontation. But it is also the place of comeback. When we repent, we do not return to where we were, we move forward into something deeper, stronger, more secure.

So, bring Him your defeat. Bring Him your failure. Let repentance do its holy work. And watch as God restores the very place where the enemy tried to take you out. What broke you yesterday can become the ground of breakthrough tomorrow. That's the power of grace. That's the promise of restoration.

7

Bethel – The Place Of Habitation And Worship

Bethel means "house of God." More than a name, it carries a prophetic invitation. It is the destination for every believer who has passed through Gilgal's cutting, marched in Jericho's obedience, repented at Ai, and now longs for something deeper than momentary victory. Bethel is not a checkpoint. It is home.

From the beginning, God has never been content with visitation. His desire has always been habitation. He walked with Adam in the cool of the day. He dwelled in the tabernacle. He filled the temple with glory. And now, through Christ, He has made His home in human hearts. Bethel is not a symbolic concept. It is the fulfilment of God's longing to dwell among His people.

Acts 17:28 echoes this desire: *"In Him we live and move and have our being."* The life of the believer is not meant to revolve around occasional encounters. We were made to abide. To dwell. To remain. Worship, in this context, is a life. And Bethel represents the place where worship becomes lifestyle, and presence becomes permanent.

There is a difference between building altars and living at the altar. Many build altars in moments of crisis, desperation, or inspiration. They meet God, experience Him, and then move on. But those who live at the altar stay. They remain available, yielded, open. They do not rush out after the encounter. They linger. They host Him.

Jacob discovered Bethel in a moment of desperation. Fleeing from Esau, sleeping on a rock, he dreamed of a ladder reaching to heaven. Angels ascended and descended. The Lord stood above it, speaking promises over Jacob's future. When he awoke, he said, "Surely the Lord is in this place, and I did not know it." He called the place Bethel. But then he left. He moved on. And for years, he lived without returning to that revelation.

It wasn't until later, after wrestling with God, after returning from exile, after confronting his past, that Jacob came back to Bethel. This time, it was not a moment. It was a move. He built an altar and called his family to purge idols, to wash themselves, and to prepare to meet God. He made Bethel a dwelling, not a detour. And that shift marked a generational blessing.

Bethel teaches us that visitation is not enough. God wants to dwell. He wants to inhabit. The spiritual life must move from encounter to establishment.

> THE PRESENCE OF GOD IS NOT MEANT TO BE SEASONAL. IT IS MEANT TO SATURATE.

Worship in Bethel is not an event. It is the continual offering of our lives. It is the awareness that every moment is holy, every space sacred. It is singing, yes, but also silence. It is devotion in the hidden place. It is obedience when no one sees. Worship at Bethel flows from the posture of, "Lord, You are welcome here, always."

Those who live at Bethel are not content with performance. They are not satisfied with spiritual entertainment. They long for glory. They long to see God move, not just in church services, but in homes, cities, and nations. They build lives that become tabernacles.

The journey to Bethel costs something. It requires leaving the transient mindset behind. No longer living from high to high but learning to cultivate presence in the mundane. The path to Bethel passes through surrender. It is not for the distracted. It is for the devoted.

There is a hunger rising in the Body of Christ for habitation. The days of surface Christianity are being shaken. Programs cannot produce presence. Strategies cannot replace surrender. God is raising up those who will build altars and refuse to leave them. Who will create space in their homes, schedules, and inner lives for God to dwell fully.

Bethel is not flashy. It is not always visible. It is formed in the quiet, in the daily yes, in the consistent return. It is a people who say, "We will not move unless You go with us." It is Moses refusing to enter the land without the Presence. It is David pitching a tent and appointing worshipers night and day. It is Mary of Bethany sitting at His feet while others strive.

To live at Bethel is to live in constant awareness of God's nearness. It changes how you speak, how you plan, how you parent, how you lead. It makes your heart a sanctuary.

> YOUR LIFE BECOMES A LITURGY. EVERY ACTION, EVERY DECISION, AN ACT OF REVERENCE.

When the Church becomes a Bethel people, the world begins to see what God always intended; not a people who visit Him once a week, but those in whom He dwells richly. The Church becomes more than a building. It becomes a house of glory. A resting place for God.

The temptation will always be to treat God as a guest. To give Him rooms, but not the keys. But He will not be one of many. He desires first place, full access, permanent residence. He comes not to pass through but to possess.

Living at Bethel means learning to host the weight of glory. Not just in corporate worship, but in ordinary days. It means cultivating purity, guarding unity, and maintaining a spirit of adoration. The altar must be tended. The flame must be fed. Habitation requires intention.

Those who live at Bethel carry a fragrance. Their lives release something that cannot be manufactured. It is the scent of one who have been with Him. It is the atmosphere of peace, the authority of purity, the joy of union.

In Bethel, you stop asking God to show up. You begin living like He already has. You walk slower. You speak gentler. You lead with greater weight. You are no longer driven, you are drawn. Pulled by presence. Anchored by intimacy.

God is not looking for a place to visit. He is searching for a people who will become His dwelling. Who will not compartmentalize Him to mornings or meetings? Who will carry Him into every room, every conversation, every assignment.

From Encounter to Establishment

Many believers chase encounter after encounter, longing for the next mountain-top moment. But the invitation of Bethel is to move beyond experiences and into establishment. God never intended for His people to survive off of momentary visitations. He desires to make His home among them, to dwell, remain, and rest.

Encounters are catalytic. They awaken us and mark us. But without establishing a life around His presence, even the most powerful encounter can fade into memory. Establishment happens when we stop scheduling God and start building everything around Him. When we no longer compartmentalize the sacred but allow the sacred to define every other space.

This is what God longed for with Israel in the wilderness. "Build Me a sanctuary, that I may dwell among them." His heart has never changed. Bethel is that sanctuary. And establishment is the evidence that we are no longer guests in God's house, we've surrendered to *become* His house.

Those who dwell at Bethel cultivate a rhythm of reverence. Their lives move to a different pace. They are not driven by performance or distracted by trends. They have learned to slow down and listen. They speak less and carry more. There is a weight to them. A stillness, and a sense of being anchored.

This rhythm doesn't come naturally but is formed by intentional communion. Those who have seen His beauty are no longer impressed by noise. They no longer rush into His presence with demands; they enter with awe. Reverence is the rhythm of those who know God by presence.

At Bethel, reverence governs everything. Time, space, speech, and even thought. Worship is woven into every step. Reverence transforms the mundane into sacred ground. And in that atmosphere, the Spirit finds rest. He comes not to stir and depart, but to remain.

Hosting Glory Requires Order

The presence of God is holy, weighty, and transformative. And for it to rest upon a person, a house, or a community, there must be order.

> ## NOT LEGALISM OR RELIGIOUS RIGIDITY, BUT HOLY STRUCTURE.

The kind of structure that protects purity and honors the presence.

David learned this when he tried to bring the ark back to Jerusalem on a cart. The oxen stumbled, and a man died. Why? Because presence can't ride on man-made systems. It must be carried by consecrated vessels. God had already given instructions for how His presence was to be hosted. It was holy order rather than human improvisation.

The house of Bethel is built with this kind of reverent order. Time is guarded and holiness is pursued. Relationships are aligned. The heart becomes a sanctuary, not a storage room. Hosting the glory of God is costly, but to those who pay the price, the reward is unshakable communion.

The Ministry of the Altar

In many places, the altar has become symbolic. A piece of furniture. A moment at the end of a service. But in Bethel, the altar is the center. It is where we live.

The altar is where the fire falls, where the flesh is surrendered, and where prayers rise like incense. In Bethel, worship is ministered. Every moment at the altar is sacred dialogue, a transaction of heaven and earth. The priesthood of the believer finds its full expression at the altar.

Those who live at Bethel return to the ancient rhythm of altar ministry, starting the day with surrender. They walk in devotion. They don't wait for the music to begin before they worship. Their lives are a continual offering, and because of that, the fire never goes out.

The Presence Transforms the Person

Bethel is the place where His presence begins to reshape everything. In Bethel, you don't simply believe in God, you begin to reflect Him.

His nearness reorders desires.

His beauty redefines priorities, and His holiness rewrites habits.

Transformation happens through proximity. The closer you get to the presence of God, the more the old you dies and the new you awakens. Conviction deepens. Hunger increases. The Word becomes alive. And slowly, the believer is conformed into the image of Christ.

What is built at Bethel doesn't end with you. Jacob's return to Bethel became a prophetic well for his descendants. His altar became a legacy. His dwelling became a gateway. Generations drank from what he built.

Those who live at Bethel understand that their devotion is generational. Every time they make space for God, they carve out inheritance for their children. Every time they host His presence, they are preparing a sanctuary for the future.

Bethel becomes a place where legacy is formed through sustained presence. What good is it to pass down possessions if we have not passed down habitation? The true inheritance is the presence of God, and that inheritance is secured when we say, "This is where we live."

The altar is meant to be inhabited. Bethel is the call to live there.

To live at Bethel is to say: This is where I remain. This is where I yield. This is where I am changed. Presence is not my pit stop, it is my portion.

We become the house of God, the place where heaven and earth are connected. Then He works through us until the whole earth is filled with His glory.

8

From Miracles To Blessing

God is a God of miracles. He is the One who parts seas, multiplies bread, heals bodies, and resurrects the dead. Miracles are woven throughout the entire story of redemption. They are moments of divine interruption, where heaven invades earth to make known the nature and power of God. But miracles were never meant to be the foundation of life with God. They are signs that point to something greater, a covenant, a relationship, a way of living called blessing.

> A MIRACLE IS A VISIT. BLESSING IS A LIFESTYLE.

Israel experienced both. In the wilderness, they lived off miracles. Manna fell daily. Water flowed from rocks. Clothes never wore out. Their survival depended on constant supernatural rescue. But that season was temporary. It was mercy, not maturity. It was provision in transition rather than the fullness of what God intended.

When they entered Canaan, the miracles shifted. The manna stopped. No more food from the sky. No more water from unlikely places. Now they had to plant, cultivate, and harvest. Blessing required participation, and through that participation, they would step into a life marked by consistency.

Miracles are glorious, but they are not the goal. They point us toward something deeper: the invitation to live in covenant with a faithful Father. To wake up every day, not wondering if God will show up, but walking in the assurance that He already has. Blessing is the fruit of alignment.

Deuteronomy 28 paints the clearest picture of this kind of life. *"If you fully obey the Lord your God and carefully follow all His commands... all these blessings will come upon you and overtake you."* It describes blessing in the city and in the field, in your coming and going, on your family, your work, your storehouses, and your legacy. It is a vision of wholeness. A vision of heaven breaking into every aspect of earthly life.

Blessing is not random. It is not luck. It is the predictable, promised outcome of a heart and life aligned with God's voice. Where miracles require interruption, blessing flows from integration. The one who walks in blessing no longer needs heaven to break in because they are walking in step with it.

> GOD NEVER INTENDED TO KEEP RESCUING HIS PEOPLE. HE INTENDED TO ESTABLISH THEM.

He wanted to move them from surviving to thriving, from dependency to dominion, from consumers to producers, from desperation to authority. Miracles are a lifeline in the wilderness. Blessing is God's way of life for His people in the land.

This does not mean the supernatural ceases. It means the supernatural becomes natural. What once shocked you becomes your daily norm. What once felt rare becomes rhythm. Blessing doesn't eliminate your need for God, it deepens your partnership with Him.

Too many believers settle for miracle-to-miracle living. They celebrate survival as success. But there is more. God is not content to visit. He wants to dwell. He wants to raise up sons and daughters who live with Him, move with Him, and carry His ways into every sphere of life.

The danger of miracle dependence is that it trains us to live from crisis. It keeps us reactive instead of proactive. We learn to pray only when the need is desperate. We give only when we feel conviction. We obey only when we run out of options. But blessing requires a different posture. It flows from consistent surrender, regular obedience, and cultivated intimacy.

> MIRACLES GLORIFY GOD'S INTERVENTION.
> BLESSING GLORIFIES GOD'S ORDER.

God promised Abraham, "I will bless you... and you will be a blessing." That blessing was his legacy. His family, his land, his livestock, his reputation, his impact—all were touched by the blessing of God. And through him, the nations were blessed.

This is the picture of what God wants to do in and through His people. Not just to meet needs, but to multiply impact. Not just to heal sickness, but to establish health. Not just to cancel debt, but to build wealth. Not just to visit your family, but to dwell in it for generations.

The shift from miracles to blessing is about alignment. It's about trusting God enough to build your life His way. It means saying yes to His patterns, His timing, and His priorities. It means putting the altar before the outcome, the covenant before the convenience.

Blessing flows from the fear of the Lord. It flows from wisdom, which Proverbs says is more precious than gold. It flows from holiness, not as legalism, but as the pathway to life. The blessed life is not the easy life. It is the established life. The rooted life. The fruitful life.

This is why God gave Israel laws, rhythms, and feasts. Not to burden them, but to bless them. His commands were the architecture of abundance. He was forming a people who could steward increase without losing identity.

Blessing always requires structure. What comes suddenly through miracle must be sustained by wisdom. Miracles bring breakthrough, but blessing builds legacy. And legacy requires systems, stewardship, and consistency.

There is a place in God where you stop asking for the same thing over and over. Not because you gave up, but because you grew up. You stopped crying for rescue and started building for habitation. You stopped cycling through lack and started sowing into harvest. That's the fruit of blessing.

When the Church begins to live this way, the world sees something it can't explain. A people not tossed by crisis but anchored in promise. A people not frantic, but fruitful. A people marked by peace, wisdom, generosity, and joy. That is the witness of the blessed life.

Deuteronomy 28 also makes clear that blessing is conditional. *"If you obey... then I will bless."* This is not punishment; it is partnership. God wants to bless you more than you want to be blessed. But He will not violate His own nature. He blesses what He inhabits. And He inhabits what is aligned with His Word.

This doesn't mean blessing makes life painless. It means even in pain, you are still prospering. Even in challenge, you are still covered. Even in pruning, you are still rooted. Because blessing does not shield you from battle—it is your guarantee of victory.

In the New Covenant, Christ becomes the fulfillment of the blessing. Galatians 3 tells us that the blessing of Abraham has come upon the Gentiles through faith in Jesus. We are not waiting to qualify for blessing through our works. We are called to live out that blessing by walking in faith and obedience.

Miracles still happen. They always will. But the believer who matures learns to ask for more than intervention. They ask for habitation. They ask for wisdom. They ask for God to establish the work of their hands, the culture of their homes, the legacy of their children.

Miracles are seeds. Blessing is harvest. Miracles are sudden. Blessing is sustained. Miracles wake you up. Blessing builds you up.

God is raising up a people who will no longer live in cycles of survival. A people who will break free from the addiction to crisis. Who will stop needing God to prove Himself and start living as though He already has. These are the ones who will walk in sustained favor, not because they are special, but because they are aligned.

From miracles to blessing. From wilderness to property. From visitation to dwelling. This is the invitation.

Live the blessed life—not one of ease, but one of establishment. Not one free from need, but one full of provision. Not one without trial, but one rooted in triumph.

> BLESSING IS YOUR PORTION. BUILD FOR IT.
> WALK IN IT. STEWARD IT.

The wilderness was a place of miracles, daily provision, and Manna from the sky. Water from a rock. Fire by night and cloud by day. But none of these miracles were meant to be permanent. They were mercy gifts for immature hearts. Blessing, by contrast, is God's plan for the mature. It is a sign that you've learned to walk in rhythm with Him, not just call for rescue from Him.

Miracles are like spiritual milk. They sustain and comfort, but they don't stretch. Blessing, however, requires responsibility. It is the fruit of discipline, surrender, and alignment. A child demands attention, but a son carries the weight of the house. Blessing is the inheritance of sons and daughters who have matured beyond needing constant intervention.

So many in the Church today are miracle-dependent but blessing-less, not because God is withholding, but because He's waiting. Waiting for His children to grow into the life He's already prepared. You don't have to beg for what a Father already wants to give. But you do have to be ready to steward it.

We were never meant to twist God's arm for provision. He designed blessing as the natural environment of His people. Deuteronomy 28 does not say, "If you plead long enough, I will bless you." It says, *"If you carefully obey the Lord your God, all these blessings will overtake you."*

Blessing is inherited, and it comes through walking closer. It flows from relationship, not religious bargaining. The enemy has convinced many believers that blessing is presumptuous or self-centered, but nothing could be further from the truth. Blessing is how God reveals His nature as Father.

A father delights to provide. He is not manipulated into giving. He prepares good things in advance. His blessing is an outpouring of His joy in His children. And when we live in His presence, we live under His abundance as co-heirs of His Kingdom.

The Danger of Crisis-Faith

Living from miracle to miracle often means living from crisis to crisis. It becomes a spiritual survival cycle—barely making it, constantly in need, always asking for the next breakthrough. But God didn't bring

Israel out of Egypt just to be miracle-dependent. He brought them into Canaan to be blessing-governed.

Crisis-faith keeps us in a perpetual loop of desperation. It prays only when something's broken. It seeks God only when the fire's hot.

> IT TREATS HIM LIKE A PARAMEDIC, NOT A FATHER.

And while God in His mercy will still meet us there, it is not the life He's called us to.

He invites us into a rhythm of daily abundance, where blessing flows from consistency. A place where your yes is so full and your surrender so deep, you're not always praying to survive—you're living to build. From miracle to blessing means you've stepped out of emergency-mode and into inheritance-mode.

Manna kept Israel alive. But the produce of Canaan caused them to thrive. Blessing multiplies what God has placed in you. It's where your hands are empowered to prosper, where vineyards grow because you tend them, and where wells spring because you dig them.

In the wilderness, nothing could be planted. Nothing could be owned. No legacy could be built. But in blessing, legacy begins. Inheritance is passed down. Fruitfulness is cultivated. Not out of fear of lack, but out of confidence in God's provision.

You were never created to simply survive the desert. You were made to thrive in the land. And fruitfulness is the sign that you've moved from merely being sustained by grace to actively partnering with it. Blessing is not the absence of effort—it's the presence of God in your effort. It's the multiplication of what's been consecrated.

Blessing Makes You a Blessing

God's blessing is never meant to stop with you. It's meant to flow through you. Deuteronomy 28 doesn't just say you will be blessed; it says you will lend and not borrow. Be the head and not the tail. You will become a source of provision, not just a receiver of it.

Miracle-minded believers always need help. Blessing-minded believers start giving help. Blessing shifts your posture from receiving to releasing. From asking, "God, will You come through for me?" to asking, "God, how can I be part of someone else's breakthrough?"

This is why blessing is such a powerful tool in the hands of the surrendered.

> IT TRANSFORMS YOUR LIFE INTO A RESERVOIR.

You become a city on a hill. A storehouse of hope. A living example of what it looks like when heaven touches earth. And through you, others begin to taste and see that the Lord is good.

We often talk about what we were saved from: sin, hell, bondage, shame. But just as important is what we were saved for. God didn't pull Israel out of Egypt so they could die in the desert. He saved them for a land of fruit, peace, joy, and power. He saved them for blessing.

John 10:10 doesn't stop at "the thief comes to steal." It ends with Jesus saying, *"I came that you might have life, and life more abundantly."* Abundance is a covenant promise. You were saved for fullness. For transformation. For Kingdom advancement.

Blessing is the birthright of every believer who walks with the Father. It is not earned, but it is stewarded. And when you step into blessing, you begin to live as Jesus did: walking in obedience, filled with the

Spirit, living under an open heaven, and carrying the favor of God for the good of the world.

9

Possessing Your Possession

The land was promised. The covenant had been spoken. The inheritance had been mapped out long before Israel ever crossed the Jordan. But promise alone wasn't enough. Canaan wasn't handed to them without resistance. It had to be taken. Possession required partnership.

God gave it, but they had to take it.

This is one of the most misunderstood dynamics of spiritual life. Many believers live with prophetic words and promises spoken over their lives yet never see them fulfilled. Not because God failed to deliver, but because they failed to contend.

Every promise from heaven requires action on earth.

What God gives by covenant must be taken by faith.

When Israel entered the land, they did not enter a vacuum. They entered territory still inhabited by enemies. Giants still walked the hills. Fortified cities remained. The land was good, but it was not empty. This reveals the spiritual warfare dimension of every promise. God may call it yours, but you will still have to fight for it. Possessing your possession means engaging in the process of spiritual conquest. It means aligning with God's word, resisting every lie that opposes it, and walking forward even when resistance is fierce. It requires boldness, consistency, and clarity.

> YOU CANNOT TIPTOE INTO INHERITANCE.

You must rise and take it.

Caleb understood this. At eighty-five years old, after forty years of delay and war, he came to Joshua and said, "Give me my mountain." It was the very land Moses had promised him decades before. And though giants still lived there, Caleb was not intimidated. He did not ask for ease. He asked for his portion. Caleb models what it looks like to walk in sustained faith. He never let go of the word. He never backed down from the fight. He believed that if God said it, it would happen, but not without his participation. Possession comes through pursuit.

The enemy loves it when believers reduce promises to poetry. He loves it when prophetic words become vague encouragements rather than battle plans. Because unclaimed inheritance poses no threat. But the moment you decide to step into what God has spoken, resistance will arise.

There are enemies in the land, not because God lied, but because the enemy knows what happens when sons and daughters actually believe the word. Possessing your possession means confronting fear, dismantling lies, tearing down generational strongholds, and refusing to bow to intimidation.

You cannot be casual with Canaan. The land was good, but it had to be taken by force. Jesus said, "The kingdom of heaven suffers violence, and the violent take it by force." This is not a call to striving in the flesh. It is a call to active faith: faith that moves, fights, declares, and does not shrink back.

Every territory God gives will be contested. Not because He is unsure, but because He is forming warriors. Every battle becomes a classroom of identity. Every confrontation becomes an opportunity to walk in authority.

> INHERITANCE SHAPES YOU
> AS MUCH AS IT REWARDS YOU.

You were not saved to sit in the wilderness. You were brought out to be brought in. The goal was never just to be free from Pharaoh, it was to be established in promise. And promise requires possession.

There is a generation that will walk in fullness. That will rise like Caleb and say, "I remember what God said, and I refuse to die in delay." This generation won't settle for safe religion. They won't trade inheritance for comfort. They will fight for the land. Not just for themselves, but for those coming after them.

Possession isn't selfish. It's generational. Caleb wasn't only claiming a mountain for himself. He was securing a legacy. The land he fought for became the land his children would inherit. Every promise you take hold of in faith becomes an altar for those who follow.

There will always be a fight attached to your next level. The enemy doesn't mind you talking about promise—as long as you never take it. But when you begin to walk in alignment, when you begin to declare, when you begin to confront what's occupying your land, that's when warfare intensifies.

But here is the good news: the victory has already been secured. God never called you to fight alone. He promised to go before you. To drive out the enemy. To strengthen your hands. But He still calls you to rise, to advance, to step forward.

Possessing your possession is not about earning. It's about enforcing. Jesus already paid for the inheritance. The cross broke the curse. The Spirit was given. The blessing has been released. Your role is to enforce what heaven has declared.

That enforcement happens in prayer, in action, in declarations, in choices. It happens when you say no to fear and yes to the Word. It happens when you stop retreating and start advancing. It happens when you let go of excuses and take hold of your calling.

Some believers wait for God to do what He already commissioned them to do. But God doesn't fight battles we're unwilling to engage. He partners with faith, not passivity. He backs up obedience, not apathy. The moment you move, heaven moves with you.

Caleb never asked for a break. He asked for his mountain. He was ready to fight giants, not because he was strong, but because he knew God was with him. That's the spirit that takes territory. That's the spirit that refuses to grow old without seeing fulfillment.

What has God spoken over you? What promises remain unclaimed? What territories are still occupied by fear, unbelief, or generational bondage? It's time to rise. It's time to fight. Not with flesh, but with faith. Not in fear, but in fire.

Your mountain is waiting.

This is the season to stop circling and start claiming. To stop repeating old battles and start winning new ones. The inheritance is real. The land is open. But you must possess it.

The process won't always be easy. There will be battles. There will be moments of weariness. But there will also be victories. There will be songs of triumph. There will be ground taken, lives changed, legacies written.

And through it all, you will discover a truth that changes everything: God doesn't just give promises. He gives the power to possess them. He doesn't just point to the land. He walks with you into it.

Every Promise Is Preceded by Process

Before Israel could possess the land, they had to endure the process. Not a punishment, but a preparation. Gilgal had to come before Jericho. Repentance had to come before restoration. And even after all of that, their entrance into inheritance required structure, unity, and divine timing.

The promise wasn't invalidated by delay—it was maturing them for it.

In the same way, God rarely releases the fullness of a promise without shaping the one who will carry it. The land doesn't change who you are. It only reveals what's already been formed. That's why many stand on the edge of promise and never take hold of it. They were excited for breakthrough but never submitted to the process of becoming.

Possession is about becoming a person who can steward that place well. Before you step into increase, God will test your integrity. Before you inherit, He will challenge your alignment.

> YOU DON'T JUST INHERIT BLESSING, YOU *BECOME* IT.

God is not slow in His promises. He's patient in His preparation. What feels like delay is often the kindness of the Lord making sure you're built for what you're believing for.

Fear Is the Gatekeeper of Unclaimed Inheritance

When the spies were sent into Canaan, ten came back afraid. They saw giants, fortified cities, and impossible odds. But Joshua and Caleb saw opportunity. They both walked the same land, but their conclusions were worlds apart. Why? Because fear filtered one group's perception, while faith guided the other's.

Fear is a spirit that opposes destiny, and wherever there is unclaimed inheritance, fear is often camped at its border.

Many believers know what God has promised them. They sense the call, they've heard the prophetic word, they've seen glimpses of what's possible. But fear has silenced their movement. Fear of failure. Fear of inadequacy. Fear of exposure. Fear of disappointment. And so, the land lies untouched, not because God is unwilling, but because His people remain unmoved.

Faith doesn't deny the presence of giants. It declares that giants cannot stop the word of the Lord. Fear exaggerates obstacles. Faith magnifies God.

You'll never possess what you're too afraid to pursue. At some point, your revelation must be louder than your hesitation. And that means fear must fall before the walls do.

Contending Without Complaining

When Israel crossed into the land, they didn't march into instant comfort. They walked into conflict. But this time, something had changed. Their hearts were more aligned, their worship was deeper, and their understanding of God's faithfulness was greater.

Contending for your promise is part of the journey. It's not a sign you missed God. It's proof that what He's giving you is worth fighting for.

But the enemy will do everything he can to tempt you to complain in the process.

Complaining in the wilderness delayed their inheritance. It distorted their perception of God. It fractured their unity. But once they learned to contend without complaining, everything began to shift. Praise became their weapon. Trust became their foundation. And possession became their reality.

When you stop complaining, you free your spirit to partner with the promise. You stop echoing the lies of the enemy and start declaring the truth of God. And in that posture, every step you take becomes a prophetic act. Every battle becomes worship. And every shout becomes a declaration of victory.

Moses brought the people out but never stepped into the land himself. He saw it from a distance. He climbed the mountain. He gazed upon the inheritance. But he never possessed it.

How tragic it is to spend a life journeying toward promise, only to never fully walk in it. And yet this is the reality for many believers. They hear the word. They start the journey. They get close enough to taste it—but not close enough to take it. Not because God revoked the promise, but because compromise stalled their ability to receive it.

There is a holy urgency rising in this generation: don't die in view of what belongs to you.

> DON'T SETTLE FOR PROXIMITY
> WHEN GOD IS CALLING YOU TO POSSESSION.

Don't be content to visit what you were called to carry. Don't spend your life wandering near the edge of fullness when the gates are open, and the invitation still stands.

It's not too late. If you're breathing, you're still in the race. And God can restore the years. He can accelerate the journey. But you must make up your mind because you will not die with your destiny unrealized. You will possess it.

Driving Out What Doesn't Belong

God told Israel repeatedly to drive out the inhabitants of the land. Not out of cruelty, but because compromise always invites contamination. If they allowed the old systems to remain, those systems would eventually seduce them away from covenant.

Possessing your possession isn't just about receiving something new, it's about removing what opposes it. You cannot live in the promise and tolerate what God told you to cast out. Whether it's fear, bitterness, double-mindedness, sin, or cycles of shame; these enemies will not leave voluntarily. You must evict them.

This is where many believers get stuck. They want Canaan, but they're unwilling to clear the ground. They want harvest, but won't uproot what's been choking the soil. But blessing requires purity. And dominion demands decisiveness.

If you don't drive it out, it will grow. If you don't confront it, it will corrupt. The land must be made ready. And God will give you grace to do what your flesh resists. He will strengthen your hands, but He won't override your will.

Take courage. Swing the sword. Clear the territory. Your inheritance is too holy to share space with your past.

Your Mountain Has a Name

Caleb didn't ask for just any territory. He asked for a specific mountain. A land occupied by giants. A place he had seen decades earlier and never forgotten. He remembered what God had said, and he named the ground he was claiming.

Many believers pray vague prayers. They carry general desires. But inheritance is specific. And possession often begins with naming what you are believing for. What has God shown you? What territory burns in your spirit? What have you seen in the spirit that still stirs you today?

Name your mountain.

Don't just say, "I want more of God." Say, "I want to see revival in my family, breakthrough in my finances, healing in my body, leadership in my city." Vague hope never builds specific faith. God honors the heart that holds tight to what He promised and won't let go until it's fulfilled.

Your mountain has a name. And when you call it out in faith, something in the spirit begins to move. The land begins to respond. The giants begin to tremble. And the grace to take hold of it begins to flood your soul.

This is not the time to wish. It's the time to war. Not the time to wander, but to claim. Not the time to guess, but to name.

Possess your mountain. It's waiting.

So go ahead. Stand like Caleb. Speak like Joshua. Step into your portion. Drive out what doesn't belong. Plant what God has given. Build what He has promised. Possess your possession.

You are not waiting on God. He is waiting on you. Take the land.

10

Crossing The Jordan–Stepping Into The Supernatural

There comes a moment in every believer's journey when standing on the edge of promise is no longer enough. You've seen the land. You've carried the prophetic word. You've walked through seasons of surrender, sanctification, warfare, and worship. But now, the invitation is not to stay, but to cross. The Jordan stands in front of you. And it is time to step in.

Crossing the Jordan is a prophetic threshold. It is the line between wilderness and inheritance, between wandering and walking in purpose. It is the final barrier between who you were and who you are becoming. And it requires more than belief. It demands bold movement.

> THE RIVER OF FAITH ALWAYS SEPARATES YOUR PAST FROM YOUR PROMISE.

God brought Israel out of Egypt with signs and wonders. He led them through the wilderness with fire and cloud. But before they could step into Canaan, they had to cross a river in flood. The Jordan, overflowing its banks, symbolized everything that could go wrong. It was deep, wild, and uncrossable in the natural. But God was not calling them to natural living. He was calling them to supernatural obedience.

The instruction was simple but weighty: the priests would carry the ark into the river, and the waters would part, but not before their feet touched the water. God would not part the waters while they stood safely on the shore. He waited for their step.

God waits for your step before He parts the waters.

This is the test of Jordan faith. It looks impossible. It feels risky. It will never feel convenient or safe. But it is the only way into the fullness of what God has prepared. Too many believers camp on the banks of the Jordan, praying for the waters to part.

> BUT THE WATER DOESN'T MOVE UNTIL YOUR FOOT DOES.

Faith without movement is fantasy. The supernatural is not a performance for spectators. It is a realm opened to those who step in when nothing looks open. Jordan moments demand trust that defies sight. They separate the crowd from the carriers, the interested from the invested.

The ark went first. God led the way. His presence entered the chaos before the people did. And as soon as the soles of the priests' feet touched the edge of the water, the river rolled back. Dry ground appeared. And the impossible became a pathway.

This is how God leads His people: not by removing every obstacle, but by inviting us to carry His presence into it.

You've dwelt here long enough.

These were God's words in Deuteronomy 1:6. The people of Israel had circled the same mountain for far too long. They had rehearsed the same fears, repeated the same prayers, replayed the same disappointments. And finally, the Lord interrupted their cycle: *"You have dwelt long enough at this mountain. Turn and take your journey."*

There comes a point when delay becomes disobedience. When staying in what is familiar becomes rebellion against what is available. The mountain may be safe, but it is not your calling. The wilderness may be predictable, but it is not your destiny. The promise is across the Jordan, and the river will not part until you move.

Stop circling the mountain. Step in.

This moment is sacred. It is the convergence of everything God has done in you and everything He now wants to do through you. The Jordan is not an end—it is a beginning. But beginnings always require endings. Something must be left behind on the banks. Egypt must be buried. Fear must drown. The wilderness must lose its grip.

Crossing over is costly. It may mean leaving behind relationships that no longer carry covenant. It may mean surrendering patterns that served you in survival seasons but sabotage you in the promised land. It may mean letting go of the familiar rhythm of just enough and trusting God for more than enough.

But it is worth it. Because on the other side of Jordan is the land. The inheritance. The territory you were born to take. The life you've only seen in dreams. The move of God you've only longed for in prayer.

Crossing the Jordan is a call to supernatural living. It is not for the faint of heart. It is for the fully yielded. Those who do not just sing about breakthrough but walk into it. Those who do not just prophesy about revival but prepare for it. Those who do not just dream of transformation but become it.

You cannot cross in hesitation. You must cross in faith. The priests could not pause in the river. They had to step all the way in, carrying the weight of the ark, trusting that God would hold back the current. And He did. The waters stood still, miles upstream. The ground became dry. And the people passed through.

What happened next was important. Joshua instructed twelve men, one from each tribe, to gather stones from the middle of the riverbed and carry them to the other side. There, they built a memorial, a testimony to future generations that God had parted the waters. That He had made a way. That He had done what no man could do.

The crossing wasn't just for them. It was for the ones coming after.

Your Jordan is not just about your promise—it is about legacy.

> YOUR OBEDIENCE NOW WILL SHAPE THE FAITH OF THOSE WHO FOLLOW.

Your courage will build altars others will stand on. The river you step into today will become the testimony that strengthens someone else's tomorrow.

There is power in memorials. They remind us that God finishes what He starts. That He never leaves His people stranded. That every act of obedience echoes into eternity.

Stepping into the supernatural does not mean stepping into ease. It means stepping into deeper trust. Into the rhythm of heaven. Into a life where the natural submits to the Spirit. Where obstacles become opportunities. Where battles birth boldness. Where every step is led by presence.

> THE SUPERNATURAL IS NOT A SPECTACLE.
> IT IS A LIFESTYLE OF OBEDIENCE.

It looks like walking into a raging river because God said to. It looks like trusting that dry ground will appear beneath your feet. It looks like carrying His presence where others only see problems.

Before Israel could inherit the land, they had to cross a barrier designed to reveal not just their obedience, but their trust. The Jordan River—overflowing, violent, and wild—stood as the final blockade between wilderness and promise. It was more than a body of water. It was a divine filter, separating those who trusted in the Word of the Lord from those who still relied on their own understanding.

Faith will always face a moment when it is forced to walk into something it cannot control.

God could have dried the Jordan before they arrived. He had done it with the Red Sea. But this time was different. This was not deliverance from bondage—it was entry into inheritance. It required a deeper level of faith.

> DELIVERANCE RESCUES YOU.
> INHERITANCE REQUIRES YOU TO RISE.

And the test was clear: "Step in before you see it." There would be no sign beforehand.

No assurance apart from the voice of the Lord.

It's here that trust becomes tangible. God waits until we trust Him enough to move when everything says stop. To step when everything screams stay. That's where the river shifts. Not before.

For those who want to live supernatural lives, this is non-negotiable. You must step into the place where you lose control—where your eyes can't see how it's going to work, and your strength can't carry you through. That's where the waters move. That's where inheritance begins. That's where trust is proven.

You Can't Bring the Wilderness With You

Crossing into promise isn't simply about getting somewhere new. It's about leaving something behind. The Jordan was a threshold, but also a burial ground. Everything that belonged to the wilderness—its mindsets, cycles, and fears—had to drown in that river. If not, those patterns would pollute the purity of the promise.

The wilderness had trained them to live on manna, to wait for provision, to rely on miracles without stewardship. But that era was closing. Canaan wasn't a place of daily miracles—it was a place of harvest. Of sowing. Of strategy.

> OF SONS TAKING DOMINION
> INSTEAD OF CHILDREN BEING CARRIED.

You cannot possess promise with a survival mindset.

Many want the fruit of the promised land while still clinging to wilderness ways. But the land of more demands a mindset of maturity. It demands faithfulness, not just faith. It requires vision, not just reaction. In the wilderness, you waited for heaven to rain bread. In

Canaan, you till the ground with promise in your bones and confidence in your calling.

That means fear has to go. Victimhood has to go. Entitlement, grumbling, double mindedness, none of it can cross the river with you. The supernatural isn't just about signs and wonders. It's about living differently. From a different reality. With a different expectation. That shift must happen at the Jordan.

Movement Breaks Cycles

For an entire generation, Israel wandered in a holding pattern. Not because God had forgotten them, but because they had refused to move forward when it mattered. They let fear and rebellion define their momentum, and so they circled. For decades. Never breaking through. Always close. Never crossing.

But the moment the next generation obeyed and stepped toward the Jordan, the cycle broke.

There's something deeply spiritual about movement. Obedient movement shatters spiritual stagnancy. It's not just about doing something, it's about coming into agreement with heaven's rhythm. Israel didn't move because they saw progress. They saw progress because they moved.

Many believers remain locked in cycles because they've confused waiting on God with postponing obedience. God told them in Deuteronomy 1:6, *"You've dwelt long enough at this mountain."* In other words: stop circling. Start possessing.

There are seasons when the only way to break free is to move. You have to walk when you're tired. Worship when it's silent. Obey when you're unsure. Every forward step says to the atmosphere: "This ends here.

I won't keep living beneath what God paid for. I'm moving forward, river or not."

And when you do? The cycle snaps. The spell of delay breaks. And what looked like forever finally shifts.

The River Makes Room for Carriers

The priests didn't wait for the waters to retreat before they obeyed. They stepped into the swollen Jordan, feet soaked, carrying the ark of the covenant—God's glory resting on their shoulders. And the river made room. Not before. Not after. The moment they carried it into chaos, space opened up for them to walk through.

That's the power of presence.

When carriers of God's glory sep into the impossible, the environment must respond.

We live in a time when everyone wants breakthrough, but few want to carry the weight of presence. But it's only those who carry that cause rivers to roll back.

> THE PRESENCE DOESN'T RESPOND TO POPULARITY,
> IT RESPONDS TO PURITY.

It rests on consecration.

Carrying the ark was no light thing. It required precision. Reverence. Unity. Holiness. But when they carried it rightly, the natural world bowed. The supernatural intersected time and space.

This is the picture for today's Church. The world isn't waiting for louder noise. It's groaning for carriers. Carriers who walk into hostile waters not with fear, but with fire. Not with ideas, but with the indwelling presence of the Living God.

The river doesn't part for spectators. It parts for those who carry the glory.

The moment Israel stepped into the Jordan, something shifted—not just for them, but for every generation that would follow. When the waters parted and they crossed over, God instructed them to build a memorial. Twelve stones taken from the riverbed itself, set up on the other side, as a lasting sign.

And Joshua declared, "When your children ask... tell them."

Every act of obedience leaves a marker. Every step into the supernatural becomes an inheritance for those coming next. The crossing wasn't just about that day. It was about future days when sons and daughters would ask, "How did we get here?" And the answer would not be theory. It would be testimony.

The Church is full of people wanting revival, but revival that ends with us is not revival, it's spiritual indulgence. True inheritance multiplies. True crossing opens doors for others. God is looking for forerunners. For fathers and mothers of faith who will say, "I'll get my feet wet now so my children can walk in dry-ground confidence later."

When you step, you don't step alone. You step with future generations in your hands. Every act of faith, every movement of obedience, every surrender to the supernatural is building something for the ones behind you. They're watching. They're learning. They're following your footprints.

The first step isn't just about you. It's about legacy.

Once You Cross, You Can't Go Back

The Jordan was a one-way crossing. Once they passed through, there was no retreat, no reverse. The wilderness was closed. The waters returned to their course. The grace for wandering was over. The era of "just enough" had ended. It was now Canaan or nothing.

And that's how it must be for the believer who steps into the supernatural. Crossing the Jordan is a prophetic declaration that there's no going back. No more divided heart. No more delayed obedience. No more backup plans or fallback options.

This is why many hesitate to cross. Because crossing requires death to options. It demands full ownership. And when you cross, you no longer get to live like you haven't. You don't get to dabble in doubt. You don't get to flirt with Egypt. The land ahead requires everything.

But that's where the beauty is.

> THE PRESSURE BIRTHS POWER.
> THE COMMITMENT RELEASES CLARITY.

When you leave the wilderness behind for good, God releases what you couldn't handle when you were half-committed.

So, take the step. Burn the ships. Cross the river. And don't look back. Because the land ahead is filled with glory, fruit, promise, and fire. But only for those who have decided: "I am not who I was. I'm not where I've been. I've crossed. And I'm never going back."

This is the life God is calling you into. Not just surviving in circles, but crossing into calling. Not just talking about revival but becoming revival. Not just waiting on the edge but stepping into the waters.

The Jordan is not your enemy. It is your threshold.

The river will part. But only when your foot touches it.

This is your moment. The mountain has been circled long enough. The word has been spoken. The land is waiting. Your legacy is watching.

Step in.

Cross over.

Take hold of what God has already made yours.

And never look back.

11

Occupy Or Visit?

There is a subtle tragedy tucked into the story of Israel's journey that speaks volumes to the Church today. After the years of wandering, the battles fought, the miracles seen, and the promises spoken, two-and-a-half tribes made a decision that would forever define their legacy. The tribes of Reuben, Gad, and the half-tribe of Manasseh asked Moses for permission to settle east of the Jordan, outside the land God had promised to give His people.

On the surface, their request didn't seem evil. They saw that the land was suitable for their livestock. It looked prosperous. It felt comfortable. And it was close enough to promise that they could still visit the tabernacle, still align with their brothers in war, and still benefit from being associated with covenant. But they were not interested in living in the heart of inheritance.

They chose proximity to promise over full possession.

This is the tragedy of those who settle for visiting what they were meant to occupy.

Numbers 32 details the exchange. Moses, at first, is furious. He sees the echo of an earlier rebellion, the same unbelief that had kept Israel wandering for forty years. He warns them that their compromise could infect the whole camp again. But they make a vow: they will help the rest of Israel fight for their inheritance, and once the land is secure, they will return to their own territory.

And Moses allows it.

This is one of the most sobering moments in Israel's story. God permitted them to settle short of the fullness. He didn't force them across the river. He didn't revoke their identity. But He let them live beneath the line of promise. And today, many in the Church are doing the same.

They want enough of God to feel safe, but not enough to be transformed.

They want proximity to glory, but not the responsibility of carrying it.

They want the benefits of covenant without the cost of obedience.

> THEY WANT TO VISIT REVIVAL,
> NOT BUILD IT.

And the result is a generation content with east-of-Jordan Christianity. Comfortable. Respectable. Religious. But powerless.

Luke 19:13 contains the piercing instruction of Jesus: *"Occupy until I come."* The context is a nobleman entrusting servants with resources, expecting them to multiply, govern, and steward his domain until his return. Occupying is not passive. It is active, responsible, and authoritative.

To occupy means to take ground, to build, to protect, to expand. It means you don't just preserve what you've been given, you grow it. You don't just survive in the land, you subdue it.

> YOU DON'T WAIT FOR GOD TO DO
> WHAT HE'S CALLED YOU TO MANAGE.

You step into your divine responsibility.

Jesus never told us to visit the Kingdom. He told us to seek it. To manifest it. To preach it. To carry it. To live in it. He told us to be salt and light, ambassadors of another realm, citizens of a superior world. Kingdom living requires a Kingdom mindset. And that mindset refuses to settle for partial occupancy.

The Reubenites and Gadites weren't godless. They weren't rebellious in the traditional sense. They were just satisfied too soon. And that is the great enemy of fullness: premature satisfaction.

There is a kind of spiritual apathy that cloaks itself in wisdom. It says things like, "This is enough." "We should be grateful." "Let's not get carried away." And while gratitude is essential, this false humility masks unbelief. It resists the fullness of God out of fear of the cost. It whispers, "Stay east. It's good enough here."

But God is not calling a people who visit His presence. He is calling a people who inhabit it. Who live, move, and have their being in Him. Who host the fire of His Spirit not just on Sunday, but every day. Who carry the ark across their shoulders, through their cities, into their homes.

The Church cannot afford to be a part-time presence people. We cannot afford to show up for spiritual highs and disappear into compromise. The world is groaning for a people who occupy the Kingdom.

To occupy is to plant roots in spiritual soil and bear fruit in every season. It is to remain when others retreat. It is to be present when the atmosphere resists. It is to carry peace into chaos and authority into brokenness. It is to govern your home, your heart, your assignment, with the wisdom and power of the King.

> GOD IS NOT LOOKING FOR GUESTS.
> HE IS LOOKING FOR SONS.

Sons inherit. Sons take territory. Sons establish their inheritance. And this generation must decide: will we visit revival or will we become it?

Reuben, Gad, and the half-tribe of Manasseh helped win battles. They showed up when it counted. But when the dust settled, they returned to a land God never marked as the center of promise. And years later, their location made them vulnerable. They were the first to be attacked, the first to fall when enemies invaded. Their compromise became a crack in the wall.

What feels safe now can become exposure later.

When we live short of God's presence, we live open to the enemy's pressure. When we build outside of His fullness, we risk building on fragile ground. Occupying means staying in the center of the cloud. Living where the fire rests. Building on the foundation of obedience, not convenience.

Occupy 'till I come. It is not just a command. It is a commission. It means this land is yours to govern. This promise is yours to steward. This generation is yours to reach. And you cannot do it from the riverbank. You must dwell in the land. Rooted. Resolved. Occupying.

Kingdom living is not a weekend hobby. It is a consuming way of life. It demands your mind, your schedule, your voice, your purity, your finances, your gifts. It demands that everything you are becomes available for everything He wants to do.

The Church must shake off the garments of part-time faith. The hour is urgent. The Jordan has already been crossed. The land lies before us. And while many still ask, "Can I settle here?" the Spirit is crying out, "There is more. Don't stop here."

Occupy.

Establish.

Fill the earth.

Multiply.

Govern.

Rule with wisdom and compassion.

Carry the fire.

The Illusion of Partial Fulfillment

Settling east of the Jordan creates a deceptive comfort. The land is lush, the flocks are fed, and outwardly it appears blessed. But there's a deep spiritual danger in living close to promise without ever walking in it. Partial fulfillment is a thief dressed like satisfaction. It gives you just enough to make you quiet, but never enough to make you whole. It's the spiritual equivalent of settling for the aroma of bread when God has invited you to eat.

Reuben and Gad didn't reject God's covenant outright. They just redefined what fulfillment meant. They measured promise by how it met their needs, not how it matched God's heart. And so they traded the land of destiny for the land of livestock. Their preference won over presence. Comfort won over calling.

This is still happening today. How many believers are living in "good enough" because they've mistaken provision for possession? How many ministries camp east of the Jordan because their buildings are full but their altars are cold? How many families settle for behavioral Christianity, but never cultivate glory in their homes?

> PARTIAL FULFILLMENT NUMBS
> THE URGENCY FOR FULLNESS.

It dulls hunger. It quenches fire. It teaches us to adjust expectations downward instead of lifting faith upward. And over time, it produces a Church that knows how to applaud revival but not host it.

The Holy Spirit is reviving hunger in this hour. Hunger that can't be pacified by nice meetings or convenient religion. Hunger that aches for the land God spoke about. Hunger that doesn't stop at rivers, resistance, or reputation. Hunger that says, "This is not enough until God says it's enough."

If you feel dissatisfied, even in blessing, pay attention. It may not be ingratitude. It may be a divine disruption. The ache is a gift. It's the voice of the Spirit saying, "Don't stop here."

When Association Isn't Inheritance

Reuben, Gad, and the half-tribe of Manasseh fought with their brothers. They bore arms. They participated in the conquest. But once the land was subdued, they went back to what they had chosen outside of God's boundary. They were involved in the move of God, but they didn't remain in the heart of it. They associated with inheritance but never inhabited it.

This distinction is critical. You can be around the things of God and never walk in them. You can be in proximity to revival, prophetic movement, or Kingdom expansion and still return home to empty altars. Association may make you appear faithful, but only inhabitation brings transformation.

Jesus warned about this in Matthew 7:21–23. There will be those who say, "Lord, Lord, didn't we prophesy? Cast out demons? Perform miracles?" And He will respond, "I never knew you." They were associated with His name but not aligned with His heart.

> THEY HAD PUBLIC ENGAGEMENT,
> BUT NO PRIVATE INHABITATION.

There is a temptation to think that supporting a move of God means we're living in it. We sow financially, share the livestream, attend the event, but never build an altar at home. Never obey radically. Never occupy the land in our personal walk. We celebrate from the outside what God wants us to steward from within.

You cannot substitute presence with participation. You cannot outsource holiness. The Father is looking for those who don't just show up to the fight but stay when the dust settles. Who don't just partner with Kingdom moments but become Kingdom dwellings.

Association is not enough. The inheritance is not for the ones who watch; it's for the ones who abide.

Inheriting land meant more than owning land. It meant cultivating it, protecting it, and multiplying it. Once Israel possessed Canaan, they had to govern it with wisdom. Build with honor. War with vigilance. Occupation is an increase of responsibility under divine mandate.

This same principle holds true in the Spirit. Many cry out for influence, platforms, or spiritual authority. But every inch of Kingdom territory demands stewardship. If God gives you favor, can you carry it without corruption? If He grants you spiritual insight, will you wield it with humility? If He entrusts you with a people, will you shepherd them with fire and love?

God doesn't release territory to those who merely ask.

> HE ENTRUSTS IT TO THOSE WHO ARE WILLING TO WORK THE LAND.

Occupation means we tend the soil of revival. We defend the walls of purity. We establish rhythms that keep the flame burning when others lose interest.

Reuben and Gad wanted land that didn't require the same level of spiritual maintenance. They wanted to live near the edge, where the demands weren't as high. But promise comes with pressure. Not burdensome pressure, but sacred weight. Those who occupy must be ready to build altars and cultivate presence.

Kingdom territory is not casual space. It is holy ground. To occupy is to take responsibility for that ground, not just geographically, but spiritually.

Psalm 1 describes the blessed one as a tree planted by streams of water, yielding fruit in season, whose leaf does not wither. Likewise, Psalm 92 says those who are planted in the house of the Lord flourish. These are not visitors. They are rooted ones. Occupying ones.

God never called His people to be spiritual tourists. He called them to be builders, intercessors, watchmen, cultivators. The planted life produces lasting fruit. It doesn't shift with every storm but deepens in every trial.

Reuben and Gad forfeited the stability of a planted life. They positioned themselves away from the center of worship. And in time, they grew disconnected. Eventually, they were some of the first to be taken into exile. Distance from the center made them vulnerable at the edges.

When you plant your life in God's presence, when you dwell in His Word, remain in His rhythms, and live anchored in community, you become unshakeable.

> OCCUPATION BECOMES LEGACY.

Your fruit multiplies even in famine. And your roots drink deeply of the River of Life.

Planted believers do not burn out; they burn steadily. They're steadfast, and they bear fruit for the generations coming behind them.

The Enemy Exploits Spiritual Gaps

The moment Reuben and Gad returned to their land, they created a breach. Not just in geography, but in spiritual cohesion. Their physical separation became a spiritual vulnerability and eventually, their region was the first to be overtaken by enemy forces.

This is a prophetic warning: wherever the church accepts distance from presence, the enemy sees opportunity.

> SATAN IS NOT INTIMIDATED BY RELIGIOUS ACTIVITY.
> HE IS TERRIFIED OF PROXIMITY TO GOD'S THRONE.

He knows that a people planted in God's presence are dangerous. But a people who live near but not within—those are easier to deceive, divide, and destroy.

Spiritual gaps are created when we tolerate lukewarmness. When we settle for ministry without intimacy. When we rely on old revelation instead of present communion. Gaps don't begin with rebellion. They begin with reduced expectation.

But the Church must close the gaps. Return to the center. Prioritize presence again. That's where the fire falls. That's where unity is commanded. That's where the gates of hell do not prevail.

Occupiers do not entertain distance. They build walls of prayer, foundations of worship, and cultures of fire.

The call to occupy is urgent. Every generation faces a decision: stay close enough to observe, or step fully into obedience. East or West of the Jordan. Almost, or altogether. Visitor or dweller.

> THE CHURCH MUST STOP ROMANTICIZING
> VISITATION AND START BUILDING FOR HABITATION.

There's no room left for partial Christianity. The hour is too late. The war is too real. The glory is too costly, and the King is coming soon.

God is not waiting for us to be perfect, He's waiting for us to be present. Planted. Engaged. Aligned. Available. He is looking for those who will tend the garden, those who will cultivate revival.

You have a role to play. A territory to take. A city to influence. A people to disciple. A fire to carry. But none of it happens while circling the edge of promise.

This is your moment. Don't delay. Don't make excuses. Step into the land. Build your altar. Raise your voice. Steward the fire. And when the King returns, let Him find you occupying.

Let Him find you faithful.

You were made to dwell in the land.

To plant vineyards.

To raise altars.

To leave legacy.

To push back darkness.

To bring heaven to earth.

This is the difference between renting space and owning inheritance. Between dating the presence and being married to the mission. Between spiritual tourism and holy occupation.

So, choose today: occupy or visit?

The land is open. The King is coming, and the question still stands: will He find you tending the field, expanding the borders, stewarding the glory? Or will He find you East of promise, close enough to observe but too content to enter?

Occupy, Church.

Till He comes.

12

Kingdom Not Crisis

The call of God over His Church is not simply to survive the storms of this world but to reign in the midst of them. From the very beginning, His intention was not that we live in reaction to darkness, but in authority as children of light. Not as crisis-managers, but as Kingdom-builders. Not as spiritual refugees, but as sons and daughters of the King, walking in His delegated dominion on the earth.

And yet, for too long, the Church has been content to live in reaction. To dwell in a survival posture. To cling to miracles as lifelines, rather than walk in the maturity of manifested promise.

> WE'VE MEASURED OUR SPIRITUALITY
> BY OUR ABILITY TO ENDURE
> RATHER THAN OUR CAPACITY TO ADVANCE.

But the Spirit is issuing a clarion call: *Kingdom, not crisis.*

The difference between surviving and reigning is found in identity. When you believe you're a slave, you pray like a beggar. When you know you're a son, you speak like an heir. Slaves wait to be rescued. Sons steward what's already been given. Crisis reveals what identity has been cultivated. Kingdom living, then, is not about escaping hardship, it's about ruling through it.

Jesus didn't come to start a religion. He came to restore a Kingdom. A realm of righteousness, peace, and joy in the Holy Spirit. A realm where sin doesn't rule, where fear doesn't speak louder than faith, and where the Spirit of God empowers the people of God to live from victory, not just toward it.

Romans 8 declares that all of creation is groaning for the revealing of the sons of God. Not groaning for more content, more church events, or more prophetic hype. Creation is groaning for sons and daughters who know who they are. Who walk in the Spirit, carry the Presence, and release the culture of heaven into the atmosphere around them. Sons don't panic. Sons declare. Sons know the heart of the Father, and they walk in it.

This is the invitation: to come out of the posture of spiritual desperation and into the reality of divine delegation. To shift from living in lack to living in alignment. God is not glorified by our continual crisis. He is glorified when we live as evidence of His nature. That doesn't mean we won't face warfare. It means we'll face it differently. We don't fight for position—we fight from it. We don't ask for authority—we exercise it.

Consider the difference between Israel in the wilderness and Israel in the land. In the wilderness, everything was about survival. Manna. Water from rocks. Shoes that didn't wear out. Miracles sustained them. But in the land, miracles shifted to mandate. They were called to build, plant, multiply, and govern. God provided through partnership. And that required a different mindset. They were no longer wanderers, they were warriors. They were not recipients of rescue, they were stewards of promise.

Many believers have spiritual wilderness mentalities. We wait for the next miracle. We depend on the next breakthrough. We live from conference to conference, word to word, service to service—rather than cultivating a lifestyle of presence, discipline, faith, and Kingdom rule. We've confused being needy with being holy. But holiness is not neediness. Holiness is wholeness. It is maturity. It is authority.

God is calling His Church out of miracle addiction and into Kingdom manifestation.

> OUT OF EMOTIONAL CHRISTIANITY
> AND INTO GOVERNMENTAL MATURITY.

It's not enough to clap for God's power—we must walk in it. It's not enough to testify about provision—we must steward blessing. Sons live in what others beg for because sons carry the Father's name and the Father's heart.

To live in Kingdom means to live above the chaos. It means to stop waiting for peace and start releasing it. It means to speak with confidence, not because circumstances look good, but because Christ has already conquered. It means to shape the environment instead of being shaped by it. That's Kingdom.

The Church that learns to live like this will terrify hell. The gates of hell do not prevail against a passionate believer.

Hell doesn't bother itself with a crisis-consumed Church. But when the Church walks in her full stature, as a bride, as a body, as a Kingdom embassy, hell begins to shake. Demons flee. Strongholds fall. Regions shift.

God is not calling us to build our ministries on survival. He's calling us to build the Kingdom on surrender. Survival says, "God, just get me through this week." Kingdom says, "God, use me to transform this region." Survival waits for the storm to pass. Kingdom walks on water in the middle of it.

That's what Jesus showed us. He didn't live from earth to heaven. He lived from heaven to earth. Every word, every move, every miracle flowed from His awareness of the Father's authority. He was never anxious, never in reaction mode, never confused about who He was. Even in crisis, He remained anchored. That's the model.

He said, "As the Father has sent Me, I am sending you." That's Kingdom transfer. He was inviting us into commissioning. Not just forgiveness, but formation. Not just mercy, but mission. That mission is not to get by. It's to take ground, expand borders, advance righteousness, and release heaven.

> YOUR WERE NOT SAVED TO SURVIVE.
> YOUR WERE BORN AGAIN TO REIGN.

Reigning doesn't mean escaping suffering. It means standing in it without losing your confession. It means speaking when the pressure is loud. It means worshiping when the odds are stacked. It means lifting your head when others bow to fear. This is the authority of sons. This is the victory of the cross. This is the witness the world needs.

Paul wrote from prison, yet he spoke as a ruler. His chains did not determine his confession. His letters are soaked in Kingdom language—joy, inheritance, endurance, triumph. He did not just write theology. He wrote from habitation. He lived in the reality of a risen Christ and a ruling Church. Crisis could not cage him. Because Kingdom had captured him.

What if we lived like that? What if we stopped waiting for peace and started ruling in it? What if we stopped asking for victory and started enforcing it? What if we stopped reacting to the world and started releasing heaven?

This is not arrogance. It is alignment. It is what happens when sons grow up. When brides make themselves ready. When priests take their place between heaven and earth, declaring with boldness, "Thy Kingdom come."

We are in a moment of divine convergence. The shaking of the nations is not just the noise of chaos—it is the groaning of creation, crying out for mature sons to rise. Not spiritual children tossed by every wind. But rooted ones. Holy ones. Ruling ones. Kingdom ones.

So, ask yourself: Am I living in crisis or in Kingdom?

Am I waiting for breakthrough, or am I building from it?

Am I begging for manna, or planting for harvest?

Crisis Living Is a Mindset

Crisis will come. Storms will rage. Wars will rise. But the real danger isn't in the storm—it's in the mindset we adopt in the midst of it. You can be surrounded by crisis and still live in Kingdom. Or you can live in blessing and still think like a beggar. That's why God doesn't just change our circumstances—He renews our minds.

The Israelites were no longer slaves by status, but slavery still lingered in their thoughts. They were delivered from Egypt, but Egypt hadn't been delivered out of them. Every time conflict arose, they reverted. Complaining. Panicking. Wanting to go back. Why?

> BECAUSE CRISIS REVEALS THE OPERATING SYSTEM OF THE SOUL.

You don't rise in adversity, you reveal what you've built.

That's why God doesn't let us avoid the fire. The fire reveals what we trust. And for those still clinging to the crisis mindset, it feels like chaos. But for sons, it becomes clarity. Kingdom people don't panic when the winds blow. They prophesy to the winds. They don't complain in pressure—they create from it.

Your circumstance doesn't determine whether you live in Kingdom or crisis—your mindset does. The Spirit is re-training the Church to think like heaven. To operate not from lack, but from love. Not from need, but from name. When sons understand who they are, the crisis loses its authority.

You don't wait for the storm to end to live with peace, you learn to build peace in the storm. Jesus did this. He slept through the winds. He spoke to the waves. He didn't pray for calm—He released it. That's the posture of someone whose inner world is anchored.

God is not preparing the Church for escapism. He's preparing her for reigning. Not a season of comfort, but a movement of clarity and conviction. The wilderness mentality must die. Sons are rising with vision that isn't shaken by headlines.

A beggar waits for something to be handed to him. A builder takes what's been entrusted and multiplies it. One lives with a need-based theology. The other lives with a covenant-based reality. The Church must transition from spiritual beggars into Kingdom builders—those who don't wait to be fed, but steward what's already been given.

Too many believers are still asking for what Jesus already provided. Peace. Power. Identity. Authority. Provision. The cross already settled it. The Spirit has already been poured out. Heaven's storehouse is open. What's needed now is activation, not accumulation.

> WE DON'T NEED MORE ACCESS –
> WE NEED MORE APPLICATION.

Beggars spend their spiritual lives waiting for manna. Builders dig wells, sow seed, plant vineyards, and train others to steward what flows. Builders take territory. Builders write vision. Builders build altars and raise sons. They don't hoard—they host. They don't spectate—they create.

God is raising Kingdom architects—those who don't just dream of reformation but walk into boardrooms, classrooms, studios, and living rooms carrying blueprints. Builders don't wait for perfect conditions. They start where they are, with what they've been given, knowing that heaven multiplies in obedience.

The Church can no longer afford to think like renters in a house we've inherited. We've been given keys, not just access codes. Authority, not just survival plans. Builders live like they belong. They expand in intercession.

The Father is looking for builders. Sons and daughters who understand that crisis is not a ceiling—it's the call to build something better. Something eternal. Something that hosts His presence and reflects His nature.

Kingdom living begins in the throne room. It starts with seeing what heaven sees and saying what heaven says. Jesus modeled this rhythm. He only did what He saw the Father doing. He didn't take cues from culture—He took His orders from intimacy. He lived from the presence, not from pressure.

> TOO MANY TODAY ARE TRYING
> TO BUILD THE KINGDOM WITHOUT FIRST

> BEING BUILT BY THE KING.

We want to take ground without first sitting in the secret place. Because you can't release what you haven't received. You can't decree what you haven't discerned.

Living from the throne room out means your identity is no longer shaped by what you face, but by who you see. You move from glory to glory, not confusion to confusion. You speak from rest, not reaction. You discern from stillness, not stress.

This is why Kingdom people are not tossed by trends. Their revelation flows from a higher realm. Their decisions are rooted in eternity. Their vision is anchored in the One seated above every name. They don't live on defense. They advance from intimacy.

The throne room trains you how to speak with authority without striving. How to act with boldness without arrogance. How to govern in purity, not performance. This is the secret to sustained Kingdom impact: you don't rush into battle—you rise from encounter.

A Church that lives from the throne room will never be confused about her assignment. Because she's already heard it from the mouth of her King.

The Discipline of Dominion

Dominion is not domination. It is disciplined alignment. It's the yielded authority of someone who walks so closely with God that their words carry weight—not because of volume, but because of intimacy. Dominion isn't accidental. It's cultivated.

Adam was given dominion in the garden. But that dominion was tied to stewardship. He had to tend, name, protect, and cultivate. That pattern hasn't changed.

> SONS WHO REIGN ARE SONS WHO TEND.

They rule through worship, through obedience, through spiritual discipline.

The crisis mentality hates discipline. It prefers emotional spikes. But the Kingdom is advanced by those who build altars every day. Who don't wait to feel like praying. Who worship when no one is watching. Who honor the Word when culture mocks it.

If you want to walk in dominion, you must also walk in discipline. You must learn how to guard the garden of your inner life. To silence the noise. To kill the foxes. To prune what hinders fruit. Authority increases as alignment increases.

This is not about striving. It's about surrender. You don't earn dominion, you inhabit it. But only those who remain yielded can be trusted with increase. The Kingdom is not built by rebels, but by sons who are under authority. Dominion flows from submission.

A disciplined son is a dangerous son because the enemy can't bait him with comfort, fatigue, or flattery. He's rooted. Alert. Anchored. And when he speaks, heaven moves.

Hebrews 12:28 declares that we are receiving a Kingdom that cannot be shaken. This is prophetic. We are not clinging to a fragile system. We are being formed by an unshakable realm. That means we can face pressure without panic. We can walk through loss without losing identity.

Crisis exposes what can be shaken. Kingdom reveals what cannot.

The early Church understood this. They were imprisoned, persecuted, scattered—and still they increased. Why? Because they weren't building around comfort. They were anchored in the reality of resurrection. They didn't ask to escape the shaking. They asked for boldness to advance through it.

This is the posture of sons and daughters who reign: they expect shaking, but they don't succumb to it. They live in alignment with a Kingdom that cannot be moved. Their peace isn't circumstantial. Their joy isn't seasonal. Their mission isn't up for debate.

You are an heir of something eternal. That means you don't just carry Kingdom ideas—you carry Kingdom substance. The glory that rests on your life is not decorative. It's governmental. It's meant to establish, to expand, to reveal Jesus.

So let the world shake. Let the systems fall. Let the pressure rise. Sons will stand. Daughters will declare. The Church will occupy. And the Kingdom will increase.

The world is addicted to crisis. The media thrives on panic. Culture celebrates outrage. Fear is monetized, weaponized, and normalized. But the people of God were never meant to echo the atmosphere, they were meant to shift it.

Manifesting promise in this age means living like heaven is already here because it is. It means bringing supernatural peace into anxious rooms. Wisdom into confusion. Vision into systems that have lost their way. This isn't hype. It's inheritance.

You don't need a platform to manifest a promise, You need proximity to the Promise Maker.

Sons who carry promise carry the evidence. Their homes are altars. Their businesses are missions. Their relationships are rooted in covenant. Their words create.

The world is groaning, and the Church is still waiting for miracles. But the Father is saying: You are the miracle. You are the manifestation. You are the answer to someone's cry. Now go release what I've put in you.

This is Kingdom, full of promise, full of power, and full of Presence. And it is for now. The Spirit is saying, "Come up higher."

The hour is late and the invitation is urgent. Come out of survival. Cross the line. Put on your royal robe. Speak with the authority of heaven. Live from the inside out. Take territory.

You're not called to just get through. You're called to reign. To release. To represent the King.

This is not just theology. It's identity. It's your inheritance.

Reign from rest.

Declare from devotion.

Advance from intimacy.

And let the world see what it looks like when sons of the Kingdom finally take their place.

13

Habitation Over Hustle

The pace of the world is frantic. Even in the Church, much of what we call faith is fueled by anxiety, ambition, or activity. We wear our busyness like a badge, measure our impact by the number of meetings, and interpret stillness as laziness. But God never designed His people to live in a hurry. He designed them to live in Him.

> THE INVITATION OF THE SPIRIT IS NOT TO HUSTLE HARDER.
> IT'S TO ABIDE DEEPER.

To move from striving to resting. From panic to presence. From religious exertion to relational dwelling. Habitation over hustle is about doing everything from a place of rest.

Hebrews 4 describes this rest as the inheritance of the people of God. *"There remains, then, a Sabbath-rest for the people of God; for anyone who enters God's rest also rests from their works, just as God did from His."* This rest isn't about inactivity. It's about agreement. It's about living in alignment with God's rhythm instead of the grind of the world.

When you learn to abide, striving loses its grip. You no longer work to prove your worth. You no longer perform to be approved. You no longer run after God's promises as if they're hiding from you. You rest in the truth that the promises are already yes and amen in Christ. You walk in faith, but not in frenzy.

This is not spiritual laziness. It is spiritual maturity. It is what Jesus modeled every moment of His ministry. He never rushed. He never panicked. He never hustled. He moved with intentionality, timing, and confidence. Why? Because He lived from union with the Father. He dwelled in God's presence.

> HABITATION IS ABOUT POSTURE.

It's about building your life around the presence of God, not fitting the presence into your already-packed schedule. It's about establishing altars, not checking spiritual boxes. It's about becoming the kind of person God can rest upon because there's room for Him.

Striving comes from the orphan spirit. It says, "I have to earn my place. I have to prove myself. I have to make it happen." But sons abide. Daughters rest. They know the Father's heart. They live from His affirmation, not for it. They produce fruit, not by hustle, but by staying connected to the Vine.

In John 15, Jesus says it clearly: *"Abide in Me, and I in you. As the branch cannot bear fruit of itself unless it abides in the vine, so neither can you unless you abide in Me."* The power isn't in our effort. The power is in our union. The more we remain, the more we reproduce. The more we lean into relationship, the more impact flows from it.

The greatest works of the Kingdom come from intimacy. They are birthed in the secret place, not in the spotlight. God walks with those who walk with Him daily. That's what it means to abide and live in constant communion. To become aware of Him in the mundane. To tune your spirit to His frequency so that even in the hustle of life, your heart is at rest.

> HABITATION MEANS YOUR MOVEMENT FLOWS FROM PRESENCE, NOT PRESSURE.

David was a warrior, but he was also a worshiper. He built cities and won battles, but he also wrote songs and lingered with God. His strength came from intimacy. His strategies flowed from the secret place.

There is a rhythm in the Kingdom that dismantles the urgency of hustle. It's the rhythm of grace. The cadence of communion. It's the sound of footsteps in the cool of the day when God walked with Adam in the garden. That's the rhythm we were created for. Not the grind. Not the noise. But the flow of unbroken fellowship.

When the Church returns to that rhythm, everything changes. Ministry becomes sustainable. Worship becomes deeper. Fruit becomes abundant. We no longer burn out, because we burn from the oil of intimacy, not the adrenaline of performance.

Hustle is rooted in fear. Fear of missing out. Fear of insignificance. Fear of being overlooked. But rest is rooted in love. Perfect love casts out fear. It anchors you in the truth that you are seen, known, and sent by the Father. You don't have to chase opportunities—you steward His presence, and the doors open as a result.

This is how Jesus lived. He didn't chase crowds. Crowds chased Him. He didn't beg for platform. His authority created one. He didn't work for identity. He ministered from it. His first public words from the Father weren't a job description. They were an affirmation: "This is My

Son, in whom I am well pleased." And He hadn't even begun His ministry yet.

That is the power of rest. When you know who you are, you stop hustling to become it. When you know where you dwell, you stop running to find it. And when you know who walks with you, you stop fearing what's ahead.

Choosing the Better Part

One of the clearest contrasts between hustle and habitation is found in the story of Mary and Martha. Jesus entered their home, and immediately, their postures diverged. Martha busied herself with service. She prepared. She worked. She hustled to host the King. Meanwhile, Mary sat at His feet, unmoved by the demands around her, focused solely on the One in her midst.

Martha was doing for Jesus. Mary was being with Jesus. Both loved Him, but only one discerned what the moment required. When Martha finally voiced her frustration, Jesus didn't rebuke her love, but He addressed her misalignment.

"You are anxious and troubled about many things, but one thing is necessary. Mary has chosen the better part, and it will not be taken from her" (Luke 10:41–42).

This scene is a prophetic call to the Church.

> IN A CULTURE THAT CELEBRATES PRODUCTIVITY, JESUS IS STILL LOOKING FOR PEOPLE WHO WILL PRIORITIZE PROXIMITY.

Not out of laziness, but out of love. Not because doing doesn't matter, but because being with Him matters more.

Habitation chooses the better part. It silences the noise and anchors the soul. It knows that the dishes can wait, the demands can pause, the ministry can be re-prioritized, because when the King is in the room, presence takes precedence.

Many of us have filled our lives with godly tasks while neglecting the God we're doing them for. We've mistaken busyness for effectiveness. But the most effective people in the Kingdom are those who live from overflow. They serve because they've sat in it.

Jesus is still entering homes. He's still looking for a place to rest. And He still rewards the ones who sit at His feet, not because they're passive, but because they understand the priority of presence. Hustle builds around Him. Habitation builds with Him.

The Myth of Momentum

In today's world, momentum is idolized. Growth, speed, expansion—these are seen as signs of success. We're told to keep moving, keep pushing, keep climbing. But Kingdom momentum looks different. It's not always fast. It's often quiet. And it doesn't originate from effort, but from intimacy.

Jesus had divine momentum, but it didn't come from networking, branding, or pushing opportunities. It came from withdrawal. From prayer. From silence. From knowing the will of the Father and refusing to be swayed by the crowd. He could move from healing thousands to slipping away into solitude without fear of losing "momentum."

This challenges our thinking. We often feel guilty for stopping. We fear that rest will cause us to lose ground. But in the Kingdom, rest is often how God advances us.

> SABBATH IS ACCELERATION THROUGH SURRENDER.

Consider Elijah. After calling down fire on Mount Carmel, he ran in fear and exhaustion. God didn't rebuke his burnout with a command to do more. He fed him, let him sleep, and spoke in a whisper. Heaven's momentum is sustained not by adrenaline, but by abiding.

What if momentum in the Kingdom isn't measured by movement, but by obedience? What if real acceleration comes when you slow down enough to hear the still, small voice?

When we live in hustle, we chase. When we live in habitation, we are carried. The wind of the Spirit is not driven by striving. It's drawn to surrender.

Throughout Scripture, God never promised to inhabit every place, but He does promise to inhabit places built for Him. Glory does not rest on the unprepared. It rests on altars. On people, homes, and communities that choose to prioritize His presence above all else.

Moses knew this. When he met with God in the tent of meeting, the glory cloud descended. When he climbed Mount Sinai, the mountain shook with presence. But he didn't stop there. He longed for a people who would become the tent. A people where God would dwell, not occasionally, but perpetually.

David shared this hunger. "One thing I ask... that I may dwell in the house of the Lord all the days of my life." He wasn't after a visit—he wanted a habitation. A life marked by ongoing communion. And it's this kind of longing that attracts the weight of glory.

We often cry out for God to come, but the better prayer is, "God, stay." Not just visitation but indwelling. Not just a moment in worship, but a habitation in lifestyle. The Spirit rests where He is honored, where He is not rushed, and where the atmosphere is cultivated for Him.

This kind of place takes time to build. It requires intentional space, both externally and internally. A heart uncluttered by hurry. A schedule that makes room for lingering. A home where the presence is welcomed and nurtured.

When we build habitation, glory responds. And where glory rests, transformation becomes normal. Deliverance isn't rare. Healing isn't forced. Revelation flows like water. Because God has found a resting place among His people.

Fruitfulness Without Fatigue

There is a supernatural fruitfulness reserved for those who refuse to live burned out. Jesus said, *"Come to Me, all who are weary and burdened, and I will give you rest... For My yoke is easy and My burden is light."* (Matthew 11:28-30) The promise isn't freedom from purpose. It's freedom from weighty religion.

Many believers are producing fruit, but it's costing them more than it should. They're exhausted, overcommitted, depleted, and dry. They love God, but they live on fumes. This is not the way of the Kingdom. God never asked us to grow by grinding. He called us to abide and let fruit come naturally.

> FRUIT IN SCRIPTURE IS ALWAYS THE BYPRODUCT OF CONNECTION, NOT PERFORMANCE.

A tree doesn't strive to bear fruit—it simply abides in the soil, receives water, and lets nature do its work. In the same way, our job is to remain. To stay rooted. To receive. And fruit becomes the inevitable outcome.

This is why the greatest revivalists in history were often the deepest dwellers. Their lives bore weight, not because of their hustle, but because of their hidden history with God.

If your fruit is costing you your fire, it's time to return to the Vine. The Spirit wants to bring you into a season where increase doesn't equal exhaustion. Where impact flows from rest. Where your life becomes an orchard of goodness, not a factory of burnout.

God is not glorified by a tired Church. He's glorified by a radiant bride—rested, ready, rooted, and fruitful.

Hurry is a spiritual disease. It robs intimacy. It distorts priorities. It dulls discernment. And it masquerades as progress. But hurry is not a Kingdom value. It's a symptom of disconnection, a sign that we are more attuned to pressure than presence.

The enemy loves when God's people are busy, especially when we're too busy to listen. He doesn't need to derail your faith. He just needs to distract your focus. If he can get you running fast enough, he knows you'll eventually stop hearing the whisper.

That's why Jesus often withdrew. Not because He lacked strength, but because He valued stillness. He refused to be driven by demand. He wasn't led by need. He was led by nearness.

The war against hurry is won in the secret place. It's won when you choose to put down your phone, quiet your thoughts, cancel the extra meeting, and lean into the silence. It's won when you prioritize sabbath, make space for reflection, and learn to walk instead of sprint.

Hurry may build crowds, but it doesn't build character. Hurry may grow a platform, but it doesn't grow presence.

> GOD IS CALLING US TO BE SLOW ENOUGH TO HEAR
> AND STILL ENOUGH TO STAY.

Because the ones who change the world are not the fastest, they are the most faithful.

From the very beginning, God has desired to walk with man. Not just to meet with him occasionally, but to walk with him daily. In the garden, God walked with Adam in the cool of the day. This was the original design: daily communion, daily fellowship, daily nearness.

Enoch walked with God, and he 'was no more'. Abraham walked with God and became the father of faith. Noah walked with God and preserved a generation. The pattern is clear: those who walk with Him carry legacy, favor, and history.

Walking implies pace, consistency, and proximity. You cannot walk with someone unless you slow down to match their stride. That's why habitation requires rhythm. It requires saying no to what rushes ahead. It means letting the Spirit set the tempo of your life.

Daily walking looks like waking up with Him on your mind. It looks like whispered prayers throughout the day. It looks like leaning into His voice while washing dishes, driving to work, or rocking your child to sleep. It is constant awareness, cultivated sensitivity, and mutual delight.

God is not impressed with your schedule. He is after your heart. He's not waiting at the end of your day—He wants to walk with you through it. The question is not whether He is speaking. It's whether we've slowed down enough to listen.

Walking with Him is the goal. Not building a name. Not completing a checklist. Not arriving at some distant measure of success. But walking. Daily. Closely. Intimately. This is the way of habitation. This is the way of rest.

We need a generation of saints who will exchange their striving for stillness. Who will trade their burnout for the beauty of dwelling. Who will lay down their religious hustle and become houses of habitation. This is the call. Not to do more. But to be with Him. To build lives, homes, churches, and cultures where God stays.

When that happens, fruit becomes inevitable. Authority becomes natural. Transformation becomes sustainable. Because everything flows from presence. Everything flows from abiding.

So, stop striving.

Start abiding.

Cease from your works.

Enter into His rest.

Let the Father walk with you in the cool of the day.

Let Him whisper to you in the middle of the mundane.

Let your life become a sanctuary.

A place where the King not only reigns, but rests.

This is the invitation: habitation over hustle.

Always.

14

From Promise To Fulfillment

Every promise of God is a yes, and in Christ, we say the amen. This is not poetic theology; it is prophetic reality. Paul, writing under the inspiration of the Spirit in 2 Corinthians 1:20, lays the foundation for a life of confident, faith-filled advancement. God's promises are not tentative. They are not up for debate. They are not occasionally true. They are yes in Christ. Settled. Eternal. Irrevocable. And our response is not hesitation, but agreement. Amen. Let it be.

Yet so many believers live in the space between promise and fulfillment. They carry the word, but not the witness. They've heard what God has said, but they haven't yet stepped into what He has given. Why? Because between the yes of heaven and the amen of earth, there is a process of alignment. A journey of obedience. A life of faith.

The gap between promise and fulfillment is not a sign that the promise is false. It's an invitation to partnership.

> GOD'S PROMISES ARE NOT MAGIC.
> THEY ARE INVITATIONS. COVENANTS.
> BLUEPRINTS WAITING FOR BUILDERS.

And the builder is not the one who creates the promise—it is the one who agrees with it, obeys it, and walks it out until the invisible becomes visible.

There is unclaimed inheritance in the Body of Christ. Words spoken, assignments revealed, mantles available, but left dormant, because no one stepped forward to say yes. No one built the altar. No one crossed the river. No one stood in the fire. The promise was there, but the amen never rose from the earth.

How many territories are unoccupied because someone assumed God would do it without them? How many families are waiting for a breakthrough that has already been promised, but never contended for? How many cities have revival locked in heavenly places, waiting for a generation who will press in, rise up, and pull it down?

God has already spoken. The yes is established. But the amen must come from someone who believes it enough to move. Faith is movement. It is building the ark when there's no rain. It is leaving the land when there's no map. It is shouting at the walls before they fall. Faith is action rooted in revelation.

Hebrews 11 is a memorial of those who lived this way. By faith, Abraham obeyed. By faith, Moses chose. By faith, Noah built. By faith, Rahab welcomed. By faith, they conquered kingdoms, shut the mouths of lions, quenched the flames, received back their dead, and endured torture for a better resurrection. These were not passive saints. They were active ones. Risk-takers. Trailblazers. Promise-pursuers.

Let your name be written in that story. Not just as one who believed in private, but as one who stepped forward in public. As one who carried the promise through pain. As one who looked foolish before they looked faithful. As one who pressed on when others gave up. Heaven is still writing the story of faith. Will you be part of it?

Every promise you carry is not just for you. It is generational. It is territorial. It is Kingdom. It is meant to bear fruit beyond your lifespan. That's why the enemy fights it so hard. Because a fulfilled promise doesn't just bless one—it awakens many.

But the process is real. Between promise and fulfillment, there will be warfare. Delay. Confusion. Disappointment. Even silence. But silence is not denial. Delay is not denial. It is preparation.

> GOD IS NOT SLOW AS WE CONSIDER SLOWNESS.
> HE IS PRECISE.

He is forming something in you so that when the promise arrives, you can carry it.

We must stop measuring the promise by how easy it comes. Often, the greater the promise, the greater the process. But if God said it, He will perform it. Not if—but when. Your role is not to manipulate the timeline. Your role is to walk in faith. To build the altar. To keep moving.

David was anointed king as a teenager, but it took years, even decades, for him to sit on the throne. Between promise and fulfillment were caves, battles, betrayal, and brokenness. But none of it invalidated the word. It forged him into someone who could rule well. The promise didn't change, but David did.

Let God use the gap to shape you. Let Him refine the motives, deepen the roots, purify the desires. Let Him strengthen your voice so when the day of fulfillment comes, you carry the weight with humility and fire. Don't despise the process. It is holy ground.

Because when the promise finally manifests, it will not feel sudden. It will feel sacred. You will know what it cost. You will know how God carried you. And you will not touch the glory. You'll lay it down in worship.

There is a promise over your life. There are words God has whispered, and words He's shouted through prophets and scriptures and dreams. Don't let them fall to the ground. Don't bury them under disappointment. Pull them out. Dust them off. Speak them again. Pray them again. Build like they are true.

Faith is not passive. It's not a "wait-and-see" kind of optimism. It's a spiritual bridge between the unseen word and the manifested reality. When God speaks a promise, faith doesn't stand on the riverbank and hope the waters part. It steps into the river. It carries the ark. It moves forward even when the ground is still wet.

Too often we've treated faith like a feeling, something we wait to feel before we act. But in Scripture, faith always moves. It builds arks, packs tents, slays giants, walks into fiery furnaces, and prays until heaven invades earth.

If you're waiting for perfect clarity before you step, you'll stay stuck. Fulfilled promises come to those who walk even when it's dark, who build even when the blueprint isn't finished. Faith is a bridge. It connects where you are to where God said you're going, and it's built one obedient step at a time.

What promise has God spoken over your life? Have you stood by, waiting for signs? Or are you building the bridge? Every time you pray, every time you obey, every time you say "amen" again, you're laying another plank of trust across the chasm between the word and the fulfillment.

God isn't waiting for a perfect plan. He's waiting for a faithful walk. His promises are not fragile. They don't need protection. They need participation.

If you want to move from promise to fulfillment, get off the sidelines of passive belief. Step out. Build the bridge. Faith walks.

Delayed Does Not Mean Denied

We live in a culture of instant results. Same-day shipping, one-click prayer requests, overnight breakthroughs. But the Kingdom rarely moves at microwave speed. God is not bound to human clocks. He is forming something eternal in people who are often impatient for the temporary.

When the promise doesn't manifest quickly, we're tempted to doubt. But delay isn't denial. It's development. God is never late—He's strategic. While you wait, He works. Not just around you, but in you. You're being shaped to carry what He's already secured.

Look at Joseph. God gave him a dream, but he was betrayed, enslaved, imprisoned, and forgotten before he ever wore a crown. The delay wasn't a divine misstep—it was divine formation. He wasn't ready for the palace when the dream first came. But by the time Pharaoh called him out of the prison, he wasn't just a dreamer—he was a leader.

If you're in a waiting season, don't waste it. Don't rush it. Ask God to do in you what needs to be done for the promise to be sustainable. Sometimes He's not withholding fulfillment—He's enlarging your capacity to carry it with character.

> WAITING SEASONS ARE WORSHIP SEASONS.

They test your trust. They purify your motives. And they remind you that God is not a vending machine. He is a Father. And the Father's timing is always love.

Stay in position. Stay in prayer. Stay in process. What's delayed is not denied. What God spoke is still alive.

Every fulfilled promise has been fought for. Even Jesus' victory on the cross came through sweat, blood, wilderness, betrayal, and crucifixion. The Church must learn how to contend.

Contending means you fight in the Spirit for what heaven has already said. It means you align your thoughts, your tongue, your actions, and your atmosphere with the word of the Lord, even when circumstances contradict it.

Joshua didn't just walk into Canaan and lounge in promise. He had to conquer it. Battle by battle. City by city. There were enemies in the land, not because the promise wasn't real, but because it was so real that hell fought to stop it.

Some believers give up too easily. They interpret resistance as rejection. But resistance is often confirmation. The enemy doesn't resist what doesn't matter. He targets promise-carriers. He tries to wear you down until you lay down your sword.

But this is not the hour to quit. It's the hour to wage good warfare. To contend with the word of God in your mouth and the armor of God on your life. To pray until something breaks. To fast until something shifts. To stand until angels are dispatched.

Contending isn't striving in the flesh. It's partnering with heaven until what's true in the spirit becomes manifest in the natural.

Living Like the Promise Is True Now

One of the most powerful ways to move from promise to fulfillment is to live like the promise is already true. Not in denial of reality—but in defiant agreement with heaven. You change your posture, your language, and your priorities to match what God has said, not what you see.

If God says you're healed, you begin to declare life over your body. If He says your family will be saved, you begin setting the table for prodigals to return. If He says you're called to nations, you prepare your passport and practice obedience where you are.

> YOU LIVE IN ALIGNMENT WITH THE WORD, NOT THE WAITING.

This is not presumption. It's prophetic preparation. When Elijah heard the sound of rain, he sent his servant to look—even when there were no clouds. He didn't wait for visual evidence. He responded to spiritual resonance.

We often say we believe, but our lifestyle reveals hesitation. If you truly believe the word, it will show up in your calendar, your bank account, your speech, your worship, your relationships. Faith without works is dead. But faith with works births manifestation.

Start living like it's already happening. Let your actions prophesy. Let your daily decisions say "amen" before the visible proof arrives.

Faith doesn't wait to celebrate. It moves like the answer has already been mailed.

The promises over your life are not just for you, they're for the ones coming after you. God thinks generationally. When He gave Abraham a promise, He had Isaac and Jacob in mind. When He called Moses, He saw Joshua. When He anointed David, He was preparing a lineage that would one day birth Christ.

You may be the first in your family to say yes, but your obedience is laying foundation stones for others to walk on. You're breaking curses, rewriting stories, and opening spiritual doors that your children and grandchildren will walk through.

That's why the battle is so intense. Because your breakthrough is someone else's normal. What you fight for in prayer today becomes the ceiling someone else starts from tomorrow. Your tears are planting harvests you may never fully reap, but others will.

God's promises are never isolated. They are multiplied across time.

> YOUR "YES" ECHOES INTO GENERATIONS.

Your faith today becomes someone else's foundation tomorrow. That's why quitting is not an option.

When you feel tired, remember who's watching. When you feel stuck, remember who's following. You are carrying a legacy.

Let your fulfillment be a prophetic signpost for your bloodline: "God keeps His word."

Perhaps one of the greatest tragedies is to settle somewhere between Egypt and Canaan. To stop moving. To lose heart. To redefine success as survival. But you weren't called to wander, you were called to possess.

Some stop in the middle because the battle gets hard. Others stop because partial breakthrough feels "good enough." But halfway there is not the promise. Almost obeying is not obedience. Walking part of the journey is not the same as possessing the land.

The middle is dangerous because it dulls vision. You're no longer in bondage, but you're not walking in promise. You taste freedom, but you haven't stepped into fulfillment. And over time, that compromise calcifies into complacency.

God is raising up a people who refuse to camp in compromise. Who keep pressing until every word is fulfilled. Not with legalistic striving, but with relentless faith. They don't stop at manna—they press on for milk and honey. They don't settle for visitation—they hunger for habitation.

You may be in the middle right now. Don't pitch a tent there. Don't downgrade the word. Don't spiritualize your delay. Get up. Move again. Pray again. Walk again.

The land still waits. The promise still stands. And the God who brought you this far is still faithful to finish what He started.

God does not tease. He does not lie. He does not inspire you with visions He has no intention of fulfilling. If the dream came from Him, He will bring it to pass. But you must keep building. Keep walking. Keep saying amen.

And as you walk, expect resistance. Not because God is weak, but because the enemy is terrified. Promise provokes warfare. Always. But victory belongs to those who endure. Those who keep their eyes on Jesus. Those who let faith speak louder than fear.

This is not the time to give up. This is not the time to downgrade the dream. This is the time to anchor your soul in the yes of God and declare the amen with every step you take. Because the One who promised is faithful.

One day, you will stand in the land you only saw in prayer. One day, the thing you fought for will become the testimony you share. One day, what you carried in tears will come forth in joy. And you'll know it was worth every step.

So, say yes again. Say amen again. Rise again. Build again. The promise is not dead. It is waiting.

From promise to fulfillment is not just a journey. It is a testimony. Let your life be one that proves God keeps His word.

15

Conclusion: It's Time To Advance

Nobody will drift into holiness. No one accidentally stumbles into a life of surrender, sanctification, and supernatural power. The path of transformation is intentional. It is marked by altars, obedience, and fire. If you want the fullness of God, you must follow Him where He leads. You must come out of comfort and into covenant. You must make a decision: I will not settle. I will not stall. I will not spend another year circling the same mountain.

There is more. More of His presence. More of His glory. More of His power. But it is not found in the shallow waters of convenience. It is not found in half-hearted commitment. It is not found in lukewarm religion. The more is on the other side of surrender. Not partial surrender. Full surrender. A laying down of rights, of timelines, of preferences, of pride. It is the kind of surrender that says, "God, whatever You want, whenever You want, however You want it. I am Yours."

This is the year of the supernatural.

> NOT BECAUSE HEAVEN SUDDENLY BECAME MORE AVAILABLE, BUT BECAUSE A REMNANT IS BECOMING MORE ALIGNED.

We are entering a season where God is restoring awe, wonder, power, and purity to His Church. Where miracles won't be rare. Where prophetic clarity won't be confusing. Where fire will fall on the hungry, and glory will rest on the yielded.

But supernatural living demands supernatural posture. It demands hunger over hype. It demands consistency over charisma. It demands secret history with God over public applause. We cannot perform our way into power. We cannot network our way into glory. It is only found on the altar.

You've circled long enough. You know the wilderness well. You've grown familiar with delay. Comfortable with just enough. But the Spirit of God is saying, "Turn and take your journey." Stop rehearsing the pain. Stop replaying the disappointment. Stop settling for survival. It's time to cross the Jordan. It's time to walk by faith. It's time to put your foot in the water and believe the river will part.

The land is ready. The promises still stand. The giants are still falling. The inheritance has not been canceled. Heaven is open. The only question is: will you go?

Will you rise in faith? Will you return to the altar? Will you let go of the lesser things? Will you stop visiting what God has called you to occupy?

This is not just a call to maturity. It's a call to movement. From Gilgal to Bethel. From promise to possession. From surviving to reigning. From glory to glory.

Holiness is not about behavior modification. It's about union with a Holy God. It's about living so close to the flame that everything that doesn't look like Jesus is burned away. It's about daily surrender, not occasional striving. It's about becoming a habitation, not a visitor.

You weren't saved to spectate. You were born again to build. You were redeemed to rule. You were set free to set others free.

So now is the time. To say yes again. To believe again. To take ground again.

No more circling. No more waiting for the perfect moment. No more asking God to do what He's already spoken.

It's time to advance.

Step into the fire. Cross into the land. Live in the blessing. Walk in the Spirit. Abide in His presence.

And let your life become the proof that when someone says yes, heaven responds.

Other Books By Nico Smit

Nico Smit has also written *It's Time To Go Up* and *Revival People,* available wherever books are sold online

Also available by Nico Smit:
Nico Smit's blog: nicosmitblog.com

www.ingramcontent.com/pod-product-compliance
Lightning Source LLC
Chambersburg PA
CBHW061208070526
44583CB00025B/3159